GAAFIL

A Careless Man

Sanjana Chhabra

Become
Shakespeare
.com

First Published in 2021

Becomeshakespeare.com

One Point Six Technologies Pvt Ltd
119-123, 1st Floor, Building J2, B-Wing,
Wadala Truck Terminal, Wadala (East),
Mumbai 400022, Maharashtra, India
T: +91 8080226699

ISBN - 978-93-5438-383-0

Gaafil: A Careless Man

THANK YOU NOTE: A big thank you to Gulzar sab for giving us the BOOK "Ghalib "and inspiring me to pen GAAFIL and Mr. Shahrukh Khan for giving us Kuch Kuch Hota Hai.

PREFACE

This story is still happening, while I am writing this preface. It is not absolute and will not be complete even after I give it an end. All stories have their ends, but this one will never have one. It never ended in 1990, it won't end in 2020. This story will not end even after the characters of the story are long gone and erased from the readers' memories. Its legacy will always remain etched in the minds of the machines (aka search engines). Though the story does not have an end, it does have a beginning. It all began in 1988, when Shahrukh Khan was still not King Khan, when Salman Khan still did not have his solo release and, when Aamir Khan was a newcomer with Qayamat Se Qayamat Tak (QSQT). The protagonists of this story are a girl named Purvi and a boy named Vikram. They meet in college, fall in love and promise to live life together. Their love is strong, but the forces against them are stronger. They get separated and married off against their will, but their love is timeless, or so it seems.

Contents

THE PROTAGONISTS

He is 43 years old and she is 41. He is Vikram and she is Purvi.

Vikram is handsome, with crew-cut jet black hair (thanks to L'Oréal hair dye), sharp features, a nearly perfect jawline and a lean physique. He is 5'10 and very fit at 79 kg.

Purvi is tall (5' 6") and bulky (weighing 80 kg). She looks sexy with her curves, measures 36*34*40* and trust me, there is no silicon in her bums. She is beautiful with long black hair cascading down her waist. Her guts match her personality; she dials 100 for every little matter.

Vikram loves everybody and everything. He is full of life and feels that life is poetry; it is to be written and shared. So, he writes. Yes, he writes.

Kahaan jaa rahi hai zindagi, Saath le chal humein bhi

Tanha hain sabhi yahaan, Kat-ta nahin samay bhi

Bhar de kuchh rang hum-mein bhi, De de kuchh lutf humein bhi

Kahaan ja rahi hai zindagi, Saath le chal humein bhi

Purvi is a cheerful lady who lives with her parents, daughter and son. She is separated from her husband. Separated; not divorced. She lives life 'not' on her own terms; it is dictated by her parents and kids. She also wants to enjoy life, get drunk, dance to good music, go out on fancy dates, but it is not to be.

Vikram's wife and two sons are his world. He is a complete family man with no interest in the so called materialistic world. He is a multi-tasker when it comes to business. He can do any white-collar odd job to make money. He can take any assignment regardless of profit or loss he might make in the venture. It just has to excite him, that's it. He says "one should never be dependent on one business. Recession can be bad and there is always some kind of recession going on in the business world".

Purvi is a kindergarten teacher at a school, and though she does love her job, she finds it very tiresome to deal with 3-5-year-old kids. Her schedule is always hectic.

Vikram's funda of life is "money is meant to be spent". He spends lavishly but also believes that excess money spoils a person.

On the other hand, Purvi is money-minded. Stingy to the core, she believes in making fixed deposits. She opines that "saved money is always good for the future"

Money has its own versions.

Vikram says, he did not have money when he needed it the most. So, he makes it and spends it.

Purvi says "I had money and it fucked my life."

Vikram is a careless man; nothing in life bothers him. He is too relaxed.

Purvi is critical of everything, irritated by everything, always complaining. Well, life has not been good to this woman.

Vikram and Purvi were both living their lives, till they meet and fall in love again. Again? Yessss! You read that right.

THE ONLY THING.....

The last time it was a BLUNDER.

This time it will be a DISASTER.

THE CONCEPTION

The alarm goes off at 6:00 in the morning. Vikram gets up half-asleep, turns it off and sits up in his bed. He chants a small verse in his mind, thanks God for a good sleep, and goes to the washroom. He conducts his daily ablutions, changes from his night-suit into shorts, tee, shoes and moves out of the house by 6:30 am. He is a regular at one of the most famous gyms in the neighborhood.

He works out for almost an hour and a half every day and this morning was no different.

At 8:00 am Vikram comes back home, goes to the kitchen and makes a cup of tea for himself. His wife, Anjali, is up and doing yoga. The kids, Ayaan and Aryan, are still asleep. Vikram sits on the dining table, has his tea and goes through the morning newspaper. He then goes to the bedroom, takes off his shoes and tee, goes to the washroom, shaves, takes a good shower, and is ready by 9:15 am. He checks the opening of the stock market on the laptop and analyses what is to be done. He sells the stocks that are to be sold; buys the ones that are to be bought, and puts some on hold, preferring to wait and buy them at the right price. At 10:00 am, Vikram has a breakfast of chicken sandwich and cold coffee. Around 10.15 am, he checks the stock market again to see if all is fine.

Vikram's office is just a few kilometers away from home. So normally it doesn't take more than 10-15 minutes to reach, even in the Delhi traffic. He leaves home at 11:00 am and reaches office by 11:15 am. Till 3:30 pm, he is busy with the stock market. In between, a real estate agent had come with a buyer to negotiate for a flat in one of the buildings he is constructing and the deal is finalized and closed. At 3:35 pm he opens his lunch box and has lunch (paneer, bhindi, two chapatis, some salad). Around 3:50 pm, he is through with lunch and lights up a cigarette. He is taking a drag when his phone rings. He answers the call.

Vikram: Hello.

Other Side: Is it Vikram speaking?

Vikram: Yes, who is this?

Other Side: I am Sub-Inspector Sumer Singh from the police station. There is a complaint against you. You will have to come to the police station right away.

The next few seconds pass in silence.

Vikram is at a loss of words. This is very unexpected.

Sumer Singh: Hello? Are you there?

Vikram: Yes, I am listening.

Sumer Singh: Purvi madam has lodged a complaint against you. Come right now or I will register a FIR and come and arrest you. Better for you if you come.

Vikram: Sir, I am in the office and it will take me some time to reach.

Sumer Singh: Come, I am waiting for you.

He hangs up.

Vikram is not a man to be easily intimidated. He has seen how the machinery works because he is into construction (wherein monthly payment goes to the police station) and finance (many ask for favors). He is acquainted with many policemen and their working style.

But this is one matter which is not to be discussed with any of those acquaintances from the department. It is a matter of self-respect.

Vikram knows one thing; any government official from any department is not to be messed with. They can misuse their powers and can cause you any amount of damage. It is always better to sort things out peacefully (by all available means you have). No middlemen required.

Vikram calls Ayaan, his elder son, and updates him about the entire conversation he has just had with Sumer Singh. Ayaan offers to accompany him to the police station and assures Vikram that there is nothing to worry about.

Na kar bharosa zindagi ka gaafil, Ye toh bewafa hai

Rijha le ise jitna bhi tu, Yeh hamesha tujhse khafa hai

Vikram leaves his office and picks Ayaan on his way to the police station.

On the way, they discuss what had happened in the last five days. The scenario was just like it happens in the movies. Vikram and Purvi had an argument over some personal issue but she made it a prestige issue and got her family and Vikram's family, involved in the matter. Purvi's daughter and son tried to beat up Vikram and abused him. They called the police and tried to file a complaint against him. Vikram maintained his dignity and preferred to remain silent throughout. The only mistake he made was that he did not file a counter complaint.

Kanhayya Lal is the I.O (Investigation Officer) in the Vikram-Purvi case. He is a 59-year-old man who is due to retire the next year. A promotiya (promoted over the years from a constable to Sub-Inspector), he has a good knowledge of the law (sections of IPC) and has experience of how to implicate innocent people in crime. He looks just like a corrupt inspector from some B-grade

Bollywood movie. He was the officer on night duty who had come to attend the 100-call made by Purvi's daughter. From the look of things, he could make out that this was some family dispute sort of case and that there was some argument. He knows a case cannot be registered for an argument; but he also sees an opportunity for himself in this entire episode. He sees that Vikram is a gentleman who has not uttered a word in the entire blame-game and feels that Vikram could easily be made a scapegoat. How could he miss that? HE DOESN'T. He takes the signed complaint from Purvi and asks Vikram to sign and put his address and phone number on it.

Vikram is still convinced that Purvi was not going to harm him in any way but Ayaan feels that things are not in his favor. After all, he had pushed a woman, which was legally wrong (legally speaking, you can't even touch a woman against her will); but Vikram had his reasons. When you are in love with a woman, reason defies all logic and morality.

This was all his fault. He was a married man with a beautiful wife and two adorable kids. He had a good life and there was absolutely no requirement for any kind of DRAMA in it. But he invited this trouble and these filmy sequences into his life and was now facing the outcome.

The other view Vikram had was that he was being targeted and some conspiracy was brewing against him. Maybe, the policemen are plotting something; the issue was not as big as made out to be. Deep inside he was not ready to believe that Purvi was going against him and filing a formal police complaint. Maybe, the cops wanted more money and hence trying to make things up.

Ayaan completely understood that his father was in a confused state of mind. He was feeling depressed and anxious because of the shockers he had been getting for the last five days.

They reach the police station.

Vikram calls Sumer Singh on his mobile. Sumer Singh asks him to wait in the waiting area. It's 4:30 pm. Vikram and Ayaan see Purvi and her daughter Ananya sitting in a corner of the waiting room. Ayaan asks Vikram not to look their way and asks him to stand away from them. He does as directed.

They are waiting for the Sub-Inspector.

In the meantime, Vikram calls I.O. Kanhayya Lal and asks him what is going on. Kanhayya Lal tells him that he was on a call (some complaint) and will come to the police station in another fifteen minutes. He says, that there is nothing to worry about. He tells Vikram that Purvi insisted on getting the I.O changed and that Sumer Singh was the new I.O who will look into the matter. Kanhayya Lal assures Vikram that he had already spoken to Sumer Singh and updated him with the entire story and Sumer Singh would help them in every possible way.

But Sumer Singh is much more corrupt and greedier than Kanhayya Lal was and he is nowhere to be seen.

After a wait of almost half an hour, Sumer Singh appears with Kanhayya Lal.

Sumer Singh is no Ajay Devgan from Singham. He looks cunning and shrewd. One look at this guy and anyone can tell that he is a money guzzler. He has the looks of that corrupt officer from some Sunny Deol starrer movie; only that Vikram is no Sunny Deol, and this is no big screen. This was real, not reel. Vikram would have taken this man one-on-one, had he not been a real-life cop. In real life, no family man would dare to mess with a man wearing a uniform.

Ignoring Vikram and Ayaan's presence, Sumer Singh walks towards Purvi and asks her and Ananya to accompany him to a room which is normally used for interrogation. They go and sit in the room. Vikram can see Purvi and Ananya talking non-stop to Sumer Singh and he wonders what the two are plotting.

After about fifteen minutes, Sumer Singh comes out of the room and walks towards Vikram and Ayaan. He looks at Vikram and Ayaan as if analyzing them. Vikram and Ayaan have nice and decent personalities that give an impression that they are not to be misbehaved with. Normally, policemen are not polite or respectful to a criminal (for them, everybody is guilty until proven innocent). But Vikram was no criminal. He was a good bait (as already informed by Kanhayya Lal) and the prospect of extracting money from him held Sumer Singh back.

He says to Vikram: Madam is really pissed off. She wants to charge you with 376.

Now, Vikram and Ayaan don't know what 376 is.

Vikram asks Sumer "Sir, how can you register a case without listening to our side of the story? Let us also tell you what had happened". Sumer Singh interrupts in between and says "listen, DCP sir is here. It is time for the drill and I have to go. I will talk to you after half an hour". Saying this, he leaves.

Ayaan takes out his mobile from his jeans back pocket and googles IPC 376. What he sees on the screen is unbelievable. He is stunned. He just cannot believe what is on the screen! He is speechless. He shows the screen to Vikram and Vikram reads the content. He is appalled. How can this be? A woman who loves you and wants to be with you all the time, wants to have a baby with you, wants you to leave your family for her.... how can she do this? He had done no wrong. An argument and a push are not reasons big enough for her to level charges so grave. (What Vikram does not understand is that the love is all gone. The woman who wanted to make a baby with him has long been transformed into a woman craving for something more than love).

This was absolutely rubbish.

He had done nothing and was being framed; that much was now clear to Vikram and Ayaan. Ayaan had been with him on the night this drama began. He was witness to what had happened at Purvi's house. But, how were they going to prove that this was a false allegation and had no truth in it. Who would listen? Kanhayya Lal had already extorted money and vanished. Sumer Singh didn't look like if he cared for truth. He was just another extortionist - a crocodile looking for succulent meatballs.

Vikram has tears in his eyes. His mind goes blank.

Uljhati hai duniya, jhoothe wadon mein gaafil

Fansa leti hai, pyaar ki baton mein gaafil

Na ho mayoos, rakh bharosa uspe

Hai sabki dor, jiske haathon mein gaafil

Ayaan pats his father's back and holds his hand firmly as if telling him that he should not worry at all. He is with him and will stand by him when no one else will. He tries to assure him that he loves him and will do all that it takes to save him from this mess.

Vikram's mind drifts to the year it all started. It was seven years back. That was when it had all started. Again.

THE GOLDEN OLDIES

(2013: This was the year when Vikram met Purvi after a gap of almost twenty-three years)

Vikram is shopping at a mall. He has just come out of an outlet when he bumps into Rupam (a friend from college times) just by chance. They used to be good friends and had kept in touch even after college. They had even attended each other's weddings. But later, they both got busy with their families and priorities. Choices change with times; sometimes it is not possible to adjust all your friends in those choices. As time passed Vikram and Rupam just could not keep in touch as they got busy with their respective lives. Now this was a very pleasant surprise - meeting all of a sudden in a mall after about twenty years. They were standing in front of each other, thrilled to see each other. They recognize each other instantly, shake hands warmly, and ask about each other's well-being.

Rupam is a tall and fairly pretty woman. Even in college she had her own fan-following with many rich and handsome dudes constantly pursuing her. Though she was friends with many boys (Vikram was one of them), she had no serious relationship with any of them. She was fun to be with. Vikram and Rupam were in the same gang of boys and girls. They used to hang out together, go for movies together and meet at common friends' places occasionally. She looked pretty and very young for her age even now. No one could tell that she was 43 years old.

They speak to each other for a while and then share their mobile numbers promising each other that they will keep in touch. They shake hands again and then part ways.

After that meeting, they start calling each other every once in a while to talk about the good old college days, their careers, their married lives, their children, their common college friends. One day while discussing about some college friends, something slipped out of Rupam's mouth. She, out of the blue, told Vikram that she had recently met Purvi. Rupam was well aware that at one point of time Purvi and Vikram were very close to each other (in college days) and even wanted to get married. Without realizing that Vikram might not be ready for this, she had blurted out Purvi's name and as soon as she had said it, she realized her mistake.

Vikram never used to talk about Purvi with anybody. She was his past and he did not want to share it with anyone.

Now Rupam was embarrassed and apologized profusely, even promising to not discuss about Purvi anymore. It had been almost twenty-three years that someone was mentioning Purvi's name to Vikram but now suddenly he was anxious to know more about her. Vikram said it was ok and Rupam could share whatever she wanted to (he wanted to make her comfortable). He even said if they can discuss about other friends, then why not Purvi? He himself asked where they had met. Rupam told him that Purvi was a family friend and that they always kept in touch; they had recently met for lunch. Vikram asked her what Purvi was doing and how had she been all these years?

Thus prompted, Rupam narrated Purvi's entire saga to Vikram.

She told him that after college, Purvi's parents had got her married to a guy who was her mother's relative and for some time all was okay. Then they heard that the guy was a womanizer and an alcoholic and occasionally used to beat Purvi for money reasons.

After a few years, she left him and came to her parent's house with her kids. Since then, she had not gone back to her marital home.

Vikram did not like the story. He felt bad for Purvi. He could never imagine that Purvi had a failed marriage. Afterall, she was a daughter of a very rich man. Vikram wondered how could they, the rich people, make such a big mistake and spoil their daughter's life?

He was feeling extremely sorry for Purvi. He could very well imagine what torture this girl must have gone through. He loved her. He wanted to make things right for her. He wanted to let her know he was there for her.

Vikram tells Rupam that he is feeling bad for Purvi and if there is a way they can talk. Rupam says she would not be able to help because their families were close and she would not like to get involved. He asks Rupam if she could give him Purvi's mobile number. Rupam agrees to share Purvi's mobile number but asks him not to reveal to Purvi where he got the number from. Vikram assures her and thanks her; he promises to keep Rupam updated.

Dost hain, dosti ke raazdaar bhi hain

Teri madad ke, karazdaar bhi hain

Mila jo mauka, zindagi mein gaafil

Dikha denge, ki wafadaar bhi hain

Vikram is sitting in office and thinking about Purvi. He remembers that they were so much in love that they wanted to get married just after college. After long last, Vikram picks up his phone and types a message on WhatsApp (there were no mobile phones or WhatsApp when they were in college) which reads: Hello Purvi, Vikram this side. Hope you still remember me, just as well as I do.

He leaves it at that and waits for Purvi's reply. There is no reply that day; she hasn't even seen the message. The next day after lunch he picks up his phone and checks if there is a blue tick on the message, to imply that the message has been seen. There is a blue tick but no reply, so he thinks of messaging her again, thinking maybe she has not recognized him after so many years. He types: Hello Purvi, good afternoon, this is Vikram again. We were together in college if you remember. I messaged you yesterday too, but it seems you didn't recognize me or maybe you were busy. Just wanted to say hello and know about your well-being. Thanks & Regards, Vikram (and sends it). Then he gets busy with his routine but makes sure to check his mobile every once in a while. The day comes to an end, Vikram goes home, has dinner and again checks his mobile before going to sleep. Still no reply.

The next day after lunch, Vikram is smoking a cigarette. He picks up his phone and writes one last message to Purvi saying: Hello Purvi, Vikram here, bothering you again. Just wanted to tell you that I am not stalking you (why would I?). I recently met a friend who told me about you. Out of concern and for old times sakes, I said hello. But if you don't want to reply, it's okay. Won't disturb you again. God bless you.

In the evening when he is going back home, he is still thinking about Purvi. She has not replied. Maybe she doesn't want to answer or maybe she doesn't want to start what finished a long time ago. He lights a cigarette and starts thinking about college days. That was the best time of his life, no responsibilities, nothing to worry, just college, friends and love-life. It was pure fun.

Dikkat hai yeh, ki hum jeete hain kal mein

Badalte hain halaat, yahaan har do pal mein

Samjhaye -samajhta nahin, dil ab gaafil

Rehta hai yeh, apni hi mehfil mein

The next day, as Vikram is working on his laptop, his phone beeps. He checks the message; it's not from Purvi. He gets tens of messages daily. Though normally he doesn't bother to check all of them, since the last three days he has been checking every message as soon as his phone beeps. Around 8 pm, Vikram leaves for home. He is driving when his phone beeps. He pulls the car aside and checks his phone; still not Purvi. He smiles to himself. He reaches home and just as he is parking the car outside his house, the phone beeps again. His heart skips the beat. He somehow knows that this is the message he has been waiting for the last three days. He doesn't get out of the car. Keeping the ignition on, Vikram picks the phone from the side console. He opens WhatsApp and checks the message.

It is indeed from her - Purvi. The message reads: Hello Vikram, good evening. How are you? and yes, I remember you. How can I forget you?

Vikram looks at the screen of his mobile not believing what he is seeing. Purvi had replied and she still remembered him. Vikram reverses his car, takes a U-turn and gets out of his lane. He drives through the colony and parks his car in the last lane of the block. This lane is usually dark and deserted after 8 pm in the evenings.

He holds his phone and starts typing a reply. He writes: The gods have been kind. All's good Purvi. Thanks for replying. You tell me, how have you been?

Purvi: All good, Vikram. Life has been okay so far. Where did you get my number from?

Vikram was expecting this question, so he replies: We have so many common friends from college. I got it from a college friend. Now don't ask who gave it because you know very well, I won't tell. I have lost a lot in life already. Now, I don't want to lose this friend.

There is silence on both ends as if both are thinking what to write next. Then Vikram types: How are your parents? Are they alright? And how are the kids? (He makes sure not to ask about the husband because he knows she is separated).

Purvi: Mom, Dad both are fine. Kids are doing good. My daughter has just finished her class twelve and son is in class eight. What about your family? How are papa-mummy, your wife and your kids?

Vikram: Ma and Pa are fine; wife and kids are great. All's great. Wait, I'll share a family pic with you (saying this, he shares a family pic with Purvi). My elder son's name is Ayaan, younger one's name is Aryan (these were the names that Vikram and Purvi had decided for their children if they got married. But it was not to be. What was to be was that Vikram still named his kids as they had decided).

Purvi and Vikram are getting emotional. Purvi looks at the picture shared by Vikram and says: Your wife is beautiful and your kids are wonderful, but why did you choose these names for your kids?

Vikram replies: I told you, God has been kind. And as for the names, you left, but our promises and whatever we shared, stayed with me. Everything about you just stayed.

There is a pause. Then Purvi asks: Are you in office?

Vikram types: No, I am in my car.

Purvi: Vikram, it is already 9:30 pm. I have to make dinner. You also go home and freshen up, have dinner. We will talk later.

Vikram: When?

Purvi: Later.

Vikram: Later, when?

Purvi: I will be free after 10:30. You can WhatsApp me after that.

Vikram: Great. I will message you. Take care.

Vikram keeps his phone aside and sits in the car for a while. He is smiling to himself, a happy man. This was the woman he loved and wanted to marry and he was now in touch with her again. Life is good and Gods are kind ....

He reaches home . Coming inside, he greets his family as always, goes to the washroom and freshens up. Then he comes to the dinner table and eats with the family. However, today he is busy with his thoughts and Ayaan understands that his father is preoccupied. Normally, they discuss various things at dinner table, but today he is un-characteristically quiet. Around 10:30, Vikram says good night to his kids and goes to his bedroom. Anjali is in bed and asks him to switch off the lights. He switches off the light and goes to the drawing room. He is sitting on the sofa and typing on the phone when Ayaan comes and says hello. He asks Vikram if everything is fine; he hadn't talked at all during dinner. Vikram is very close to Ayaan and he doesn't want to lie to him, so he tells him about Purvi. Ayaan says its ok to have friends but advises him not to tell mother about this because she wouldn't like it. Then he says good night and leaves. Vikram messages Purvi on WhatsApp. Purvi replies that she's having dinner with the family and that she will message him tomorrow. They say good night and bid goodbye.

Vikram is in his bed trying to sleep when the phone beeps. He is in no mood to check who is messaging. After some time, the phone beeps again. Then again. Then again. Finally, he gets up and checks who is messaging at this time. Even Anjali's sleep is disturbed and she asks who is messaging him at this time. She asks him to shut the phone and sleep. Still, Vikram checks the phone and sees it is Purvi. She has messaged 'hello' five times. Vikram doesn't want to disturb Anjali; so, he moves out of the bedroom and goes to the drawing room again, and replies to Purvi's message: Hello, you are still awake ....?

Purvi: Dinner was late today. Then it took time to wind up the kitchen. I could come to my bedroom only now. Then thought, let me WhatsApp you. Anyways, it is late now. You go and sleep. We will talk tomorrow. Good night ...

Vikram knows its late, and she has school in the morning, so he says good night and goes back to his bedroom. Anjali hasn't slept yet. She asks him whose message it was, and Vikram replies: It was Verma (friend from college days). This was the first time that Vikram had lied to Anjali, and this was just the beginning. After that day, whenever Vikram was busy on the phone (with Purvi) and Anjali asked who he was messaging or talking to, he would always take the name of a friend who Anjali didn't know. He didn't want to tell her; he didn't want to hurt her. Which woman would bear the pain of her husband being friends with a woman he loved in college years? So, he decided that he would not tell Anjali.

He was happy and thanking the Gods that he was again in touch with Purvi. Lying on the bed, not once did it come to his mind, that he was a happily married man with two teenage kids and that his wife was sleeping by his side.

Waqt badalta hai, log badal jaate hain gaafil ....

Soch badalti hai, rishte badal jaate hain gaafil ....

Nahin badalte hain, toh dilon ke ehsaas ....

Woh wahin, theher jaate hain gaafil ....

Next day Vikram is in office. Around 2:30 pm. he gets a message from Purvi: Hello, good afternoon. How are you?

Vikram is busy, but still, he checks the message. It is Purvi's. Vikram smiles and replies: Hello, good afternoon, I'm good, how are you?

Purvi: I'm fine; coming back home from school in the school bus so thought of messaging you. What are you doing right now?

Vikram: Good thought. I'm in my office, working.

Purvi: Sorry I'm disturbing you. Please continue with your work; we will chat after lunch. Bye.

Vikram: Okay. You also take some rest; you must be tired. We will talk around 4:00 pm. Bye.

Vikram finishes his work, has lunch, lights up a cigarette. Just then, his phone beeps. It's 4:00 pm.

Purvi: Good evening, how are you?

Vikram: Good evening, can I call? We have only been messaging. This typing takes a lot of time. So, can we talk instead?

Purvi: Same here Vikram, but for now, we will message. I will tell you when we can talk. (She pauses for a few seconds and then types) Now, I'm going to rest for some time, then do some school work, followed by dinner preparation. I'll message you after that. Till then, you be busy with your work. We will talk around 10:00. Bye.

This late-night messaging was risky. Already Ayaan had enquired and Anjali had questioned (a change in behavioural pattern can easily be noticed by anybody), but Vikram was ready to take the risk, not knowing that this was going to become a bad habit, and cause trouble for him one day.

At 10 pm, Purvi messages Vikram: Hello. I'm through with dinner and am in my room. If you want to talk, you can call now. (On getting no response from Vikram's side, she resends the same message).

Vikram is sitting with his kids and they are having a normal conversation about their school and college. Anjali tells him that there's some message beeping on his phone. Vikram goes and checks the message. It is Purvi; she wants to talk. His heart beats faster. How can he talk to her in front of everybody? So, he decides to go for a walk and talk. He asks Anjali and the kids if they want to go for a walk, but they are not interested, so he moves out alone, smiling and thanking the Gods that none came along.

Once outside, he messages Purvi: Shall I call you?

Purvi: Wait, I will call. (She calls)

Vikram picks up on the first ring, (he can hear his heartbeat in the phone) and says: Hello.

Purvi: Hello ... (pause of a few seconds). How are you? (her voice is also over-excited and emotional).

Vikram is almost in tears; he is hearing her voice after 23 years. He somehow manages a smile on his face. It's a wonderful feeling. He is so happy that he is finally talking to her. (They used to talk for hours when in college, and suddenly it all stopped. No bye-byes, no clarifications, just a full-stop to all conversations and meetings and promises). Vikram wants to tell Purvi that he still loves her, but manages a simple: I'm fine. Then he pauses and says: It's been so long. I was thinking you must have changed, but you still have that lovely voice, and now it seems as if it was yesterday that we were talking on the phone.

Purvi: Just that there were no mobile phones then. Only land lines. And we were not permitted to talk (sounds sad).

Saying this, she changes the topic and says, tell me, how is your life going? How is your family, your business?

Vikram wants to discuss a lot of things with her, the times they were together, the times they were separated, the times they got married ... everything he wanted to know and tell.

But Purvi is more interested in his story ...so she asks him again: Don't you want to tell ...?

Vikram: There's so much to tell, but this is not the time to discuss those stories. I will sit with you and we will talk, face to face. I want to meet you. When can we meet?

Purvi: Vikram, meeting is not possible. You know I'm working and I'm staying with my parents, and I have kids too. I have to manage a lot of things, so meeting is not possible. But yes, we can talk, we can message. We can share our stories on phone.

Vikram wants to see her for once, so he asks: Okay, fine. We will not meet. But I want to see you just once. It's been years, I haven't seen you. So, tell me, when can I come and see you? I can come right now. (Vikram is serious. In college years, he used to go to Purvi's colony just to see her, whenever they could not meet. It was a routine they both religiously followed. Five honks of his bike horn and she would come to the gate of her house to see him, say hi and bye).

Purvi very well knows that he is not going to relent. She knows he loved her a lot. She knows he still loves her. Otherwise, who would remember a girl after these many years? With time, people forget. People have short and weak memories. They move on creating new memories and deleting the old ones. But Vikram and Purvi were both different. They had not forgotten each other. They both still loved those old images they had in their minds of each other.

So, she says that he could see her the next day and that he should now go home and sleep.

RENDEZVOUS

Vikram could not sleep well that night. He was well awake till 2 am, thinking about Purvi and himself. Those were beautiful days ... and then they were gone in a flash. What remained were painful memories, which he could share with no one, tell no one. And now, Purvi was back. Back for good or bad, he did not know, but she was back, and he was happy. Deep inside, after their separation, he knew he would meet her one day. He knew that his story was not over yet. He knew that the Gods would be kind enough to make him meet her one day. What he did not know was that it was going to take twenty-three years ....

The next day, Vikram messages Purvi at around 2:30 in the afternoon, when she is coming back from school. He reminds her that he would be coming to see her in the evening. She is in a playful mood. Teasingly, she says she won't be able to come to the gate in the evening; that someone might see them meeting. She knows Vikram is going to feel bad about this, but she says it purposely, wanting to check what he says next. Vikram says that he's going to come as he always used to in earlier times, and it is up to her whether she wants to come to the gate or not. This is exactly what Purvi loved about him then, and now he was acting just the same. She asks him why he wants to come. He answers, just to see her. She asks what he wants to check and he says if she's still that beautiful. She asks what he will achieve by doing that and he replies, inner peace. She smiles, he smiles ....

In the evening, Vikram leaves his office early. He has messaged Purvi, telling her that he will reach her place in 20 minutes. Purvi replies that she will call in 10 minutes. Vikram is driving when she calls. Vikram puts his phone on speaker mode and says hello. Purvi tells him not to honk his car horn when he reaches her house. Instead, he has to give a missed call on her mobile. She asks him to stop his car a little further down the lane and wait for her.

Vikram reaches her colony, passes the colony temple, and stops his car. (This is the same spot where he used to stop his bike.) He folds his hands, prays for a second and then gives Purvi a missed call. Her house is just 300 metres away. A 500-yard kothi, which only rich people can afford in Delhi, even in today's times. Her father was a rich man having a big house, an expensive car, and two factories in those days. He remembers everything about her and her family. What make of car her father used to drive, what was the car's number, what was the landline phone number, the kothi number. He hadn't forgotten anything. It was just like yesterday, and now, coming to her colony after almost 23 years, it was a trip down memory lane. Vikram gets emotional and smiles to himself, tears in his eyes.

He stops on the side of house no. 116. It's a corner house with its front on the left side. Purvi calls and confirms if he has reached and asks his car number. She comes out of her house and walks towards Vikram's car. Vikram has been constantly watching the rear-view mirror of his car. He sees her coming and his heartbeat goes for a toss. He just can't believe what he is seeing in the rear-view mirror. Purvi is still as beautiful as she was then. She comes to the left side of the car, looks in the car window, smiles, and says hello to Vikram. In a flash of a second, Vikram is out of his car. He wants to reach out to her and hug her, but instead, he stands still, just staring at her with a big grin on his face. He is seeing her for the first time in 23 years. 23 long years. She's still very pretty; the mole on her left cheek still makes her look sexy. There are black circles under her eyes, but the glow of her skin (silky smooth) is still the same. She's a bit heavier (around 80kg), but because of her height (5 feet 6 inches), she doesn't look fat. She still has a good figure (has one of the best backs one could get to see) and is in good shape. She's wearing a baby pink half sleeve tee-shirt with black jogging pants. She says hello again. Vikram is still at loss of words, not believing that Purvi, in real, is standing in front of him. He is overwhelmed with joy. This was the girl he wanted to get married to (but could not). They had lost all contact, had no knowledge of each other's whereabouts for 23 years, and were now standing in front of each other, face to face. This was no movie, no tragic song was playing in the background, and they were not embracing each other and crying. This was real life and they were standing eight feet apart, on either side of the car, just smiling at each other. None uttering a word.

Yeh mohabbat bhi, kya cheez hai gaafil ....

Mil ke bichhad jayen, toh bahaana ban jaata hai ....

Bichhad ke mil jayen, toh afsaana ban jaata hai ....

Finally, Purvi says: Happy to see me? Now I have to go.... Vikram interrupts and asks, when do we meet again? Purvi says: Have patience. We will meet. I will let you know very soon. Okay? Now bye ... She turns and starts walking towards her house. Vikram sees her going away. She still has a wonderful walk.

For him, the story begins again from where it seemed to have ended. He feels like he is still 20 years old; his mind says: You are still in 1990, and the 23 years between 1990-2013 just didn't happen. This was the girl he loved. She might be a 41-year-old woman, but for him, she was still that 18-year-old girl. Immersed in these thoughts, Vikram sits in the car and drives away....

THE CONNECT

Over the next few days, Purvi and Vikram talk about their college days. How they met and how they fell in love. The time spent in the classroom, the college canteen, which movies they saw together, which restaurant they used to go and sit for coffee, how once she had eaten a bowl full of chillies just to express her love for him, how once he had taken her for an Anil Kapoor-Madhuri Dixit movie and it turned out to be a Sanjeev Kumar flopper with just two of them in the theatre. How she was scared to sit with him on his bike, how they used to hold hands and go for long walks, how they enjoyed walking in the rains. They also discussed about their college friends and who all were in touch and how their lives were now. Nowadays, Vikram and Purvi are constantly on the phone, messaging and calling each other at regular intervals (taking a break only when Purvi is in school or Vikram is busy with a client). The only thing they both have avoided till now is discussing their lives after their break-up in college.

One fine day, Purvi tells Vikram, that her parents are going for a holiday to South Africa with her elder sister Anita and her husband Vivek. They would be gone for almost a week. So, she says that the day her parents fly, she and Vikram can meet up. They can go for a drive, or for lunch, or coffee or whatever. This is what he wanted, to meet. So, she tells him the exact day, which is the day after tomorrow and asks him to pick her up from a given point, as she would be coming by the school bus after the school. The programme is finalized and they are meeting again. Both of them are happy and excited like teenagers. Purvi asks Vikram if he would take her for lunch, or if they were going for a movie, or would they just sit in the car and talk? He says they will go to some decent place for lunch and sit and talk.

Next day Purvi is busy packing and getting things ready for her parents' trip. She also makes sure to finish all her pending work at home and school, because she is to meet Vikram tomorrow in the afternoon, and would be out for the whole day.

Purvi had told her daughter Ananya about Vikram, the day she received the first WhatsApp message from him. She had told her that they were very good friends in college and wanted to marry each other, but for Nanu (maternal grandfather), who was against their relationship and got her married to Ramit instead. The rest, Ananya knows all about how her mother's (Purvi's) marriage went bad.

So, on Thursday, before going to school, Purvi tells Ananya that she is going to meet Vikram after school and that they would be going for lunch and she would be coming late in the evening (the parents had taken the early morning flight to Cape Town). Ananya has just finished her class Twelve and is due to take admission in college. Purvi's son, Chhotu, has already gone to school (he is in class Eight). Purvi tells Ananya, that the lunch has already been prepared and everything is in the refrigerator. She just has to microwave it all and if there are any problems, she can call her on mobile. Saying thus, Purvi bids bye to Ananya and leaves for school.

Vikram gets ready as usual and leaves for office on time. He knows he has to wind up work early as he has to pick Purvi up at 2:45. He finishes all pending work by 2:30 and leaves for the designated pickup point. He reaches there on time and barely has to wait for a minute when Purvi's school bus arrives. She gets down from the bus and sees Vikram's car parked just ahead. She comes and sits in the car, smiles and says hello. Vikram also smiles and says hello to her.

Finally, they are together again. Now Purvi is sitting in Vikram's car but she never sat on Vikram's bike when in college; not even once. She used to say that she was afraid of sitting with him on his monster bike. Vikram loved his bike as much as he loved her (as all youngsters of his age did), and kept it (bike) even after Purvi was long gone. Whenever or wherever they used to go, they always took an autorickshaw. Those were the days. He couldn't afford a car then, but now he does.

Purvi is wearing a green suit and is looking very pretty. The dark circles under her eyes have somehow vanished. On the way, they discuss what kind of food they would like to have for lunch (Chinese, Mexican, Thai, Mughlai, Italian), and they finally settle for Indian Mughlai. They are the true Punjabis ... she loves her Butter Chicken, and he loves his Dal Bukhara. Vikram takes Purvi to an upscale market, parks his car, and they start looking for a good Indian restaurant. This market is all about good restaurants and good food. Vikram and Purvi decide to go to an Indian restaurant famous for their chicken gravies and special dal. They go inside and take a corner table. the restaurant is dimly lit and some soft instrumental music is playing in the backdrop. Since it is a bit late for lunch (it is already 3:15 pm), only one other table on the other end is occupied by a young couple. The waiter comes with the bar menu and the food menu and asks if they would like to have bottled water or normal water. Purvi asks him to give bottled water and thanks him.

Vikram asks Purvi if she would like to have beer and she nods in the affirmative. He orders two bottles of chilled beer. The waiter serves it in two beer glasses, along with some peanuts and wafers. Vikram asks if Purvi would like to have some snacks and she says no. She orders the food and tells the waiter that food should be served only when they are through with the beer.

Purvi loves hard drinks and has a good appetite for fancy food. She says cheers and takes a sip from her glass. The beer is chilled and she likes it. She is in a good mood and so is Vikram. Purvi smiles at him and he is thinking where to start the conversation from. He smiles back. They are quiet for a few seconds and then Purvi asks Vikram to say something. He (as if waiting for this opportunity) says: I have missed you a lot all these years. It's good to be sitting here with you and enjoying the beer, but this is what I had wanted for us, always. To be with you, having lunches and dinners with you, go on long drives with you, go on holidays, have a family and a decent life with you. He smiles wryly.

Purvi wanted the same life, but it did not happen. She bottoms-ups the glass and keeps it on the table. Then she says: You know what Vikram, it was all your fault. You did not try hard enough. You should have been more courageous; you should have pursued me more passionately. You should have talked my parents into getting us married. They wouldn't have refused. After all, their two elder daughters were married into middle class families. You should have at least tried. But no; you just gave in to the pressure of me belonging to a very rich family, and that my father was never going to say yes. He would have, but you just didn't have the guts. She smiles dryly.

Vikram is now feeling sorry for her and for himself. How could he make her believe that he tried - tried hard enough - but her father was totally against their relationship. That her father had met his father and conveyed that they were no match for their family in terms of status and money. The meeting had been a complete disaster. A disaster which resulted in both of them getting married the very next year to somebody else and not each other. (Vikram finishes his beer and beckons to the waiter to serve the food).

The food is served and they enjoy the delicacies ...Quietly.

Its 4:30 pm, and they are through with lunch. The waiter asks if they would like to have something in desserts, to which Purvi says, 'no, thank you'. Vikram asks the waiter to get the bill and pays in cash. He thanks the waiter and leaves some cash as tip. Then Purvi and Vikram come out of the restaurant and walk towards the parking lot. They sit in the car, pay the parking guy and drive out of the market. Vikram asks Purvi if she wants to have some ice-cream or coffee at some other place. She replies that they had just had lunch, so she wouldn't have anything for now.

Vikram: Did you like the food?

Purvi: It was awesome.

Vikram: Where do you want to go now?

Purvi: I don't want to go home so early. I have told Ananya that I will be coming back late. So, it is up to you, where you want to take me.

This was one thing Vikram loved about Purvi. Even when they were in college, and whenever they used to meet out of the college, she would never be in a hurry to leave. In fact, she never wanted to go home. It was always Vikram who would ask her to go on time so that nobody at home questioned her whereabouts.

They drive towards India Gate. Purvi holds Vikram's hand and asks him to just drive. He can feel the warmth of her hand on his. This was not the first time she was holding his hand. They used to hold hands and talk for hours in college days. They reach India Gate and Vikram parks his car on the sides of the lawns. They sit in the car for around half an hour, just holding hands, gazing at each other, feeling each other's presence, letting it soak in that they are finally together once again.

After some time, Purvi asks Vikram if he wants to walk on the lawns with her. He happily agrees. They stroll on the lawns for around an hour, holding hands, not talking much (as if on a college date). They are enjoying each other's company. At around 7:00 pm, they stop for ice-cream, and share a Choco-chip cup. It is getting dark; Vikram asks Purvi if they should leave for home now.

On the way back, Purvi tells Vikram that she has told her daughter Ananya about him and that Ananya is excited and wants to meet him. Vikram says he is ready to meet her whenever she wants to. Purvi is again holding Vikram's hand. They reach Purvi's house. She gives him a hug (he can smell her body's fragrance, which is very sexy). Then she kisses him on his cheek, says bye, gets down from the car and goes inside the gate. He watches her going inside, her fragrance still lingering in his nostrils. He doesn't want her to go but what to do? He smiles, and drives away.

Yeh shaam bahut rangeen thee gaafil ....

Tum pehle se zyada, haseen theen gaafil ...

kya sunayen ab tumhein, haal-e-dil apna ....

Zindagi bin tumhare, gamgeen thee gaafil ....

NO COMMITMENTS

Two days later, on Saturday around 12:00 in the noon, Purvi calls Vikram and asks him if he is free in the evening. She says that she and Ananya are going for shopping and asks if he can join them there. Vikram knew he had to meet Ananya, so he says it's okay with him and that he will meet them around 7:00 pm. In the evening at around 6:00 pm, he leaves office and goes home, freshens-up, has tea with Anjali and asks her if she wants to go shopping with him. She says she has to go for a kitty dinner. So Vikram asks his kids if they want to go with him. Ayaan is ready but Aryan says he has to go out with friends. At 6:45 pm, Anjali leaves for her kitty dinner and Vikram and Ayaan for the shopping mall.

On the way, Vikram gives a short background story of himself and Purvi to Ayaan (the college stuff and the breakup and how they have met after 23 years). Ayaan is a sensible boy. He doesn't mind his father having women friends (he knows a few of them actually), and he knows his father very well (he's the closest to him). He's a man who would do no harm to anybody in any way and will always stand for anybody who needs his help.

They reach the mall and Vikram calls Purvi to ask her where they are. Purvi says they were through with their shopping and going to the coffee shop. Vikram parks the car in the basement and then he and Ayaan take the escalator to the ground floor and walk towards the coffee shop. They enter the café and see Purvi and Ananya sitting at a corner table (corner tables are always good for long conversations). They go and join them. Purvi and Ananya greet Vikram and Ayaan (they all shake hands). Vikram introduces Ayaan to Purvi and Ananya, and Purvi introduces Ananya to Vikram and Ayaan. Vikram goes to the counter and orders four cold coffees, some cookies and cakes. He then goes back to the table and sits with them. Ananya and Ayaan get talking instantly, as if they have been friends for long. They discuss about good colleges, college admissions, courses and cut-offs (Ayaan is in second year of college and Ananya has yet to take admission). Purvi is happy that Vikram has brought his son along. The coffee, cookies and cake arrive and they all start enjoying, along with the conversation.

Ananya is a girl who has spent her entire childhood away from her father, at her maternal grandparents' house, deprived of a father's love. She very well knows that her father left them when she was just six years old (and her brother barely six months old) and vanished. She does meet her father sometimes now, but that is just because her parents are not divorced and also because her father wants to remain in touch, just for the sake of it (or maybe because of the money and property Purvi is going to inherit from her parents). There is no bonding, no love. The guy doesn't even pay their school fees on time (let alone bear the other expenses of his two kids), which he had promised he always will.

Ananya looks at Vikram and then her mother and has a feeling that maybe, this man is going to marry her mother and take care of them all. (Take care of them, definitely he will, but marriage, is that possible?)

Ananya asks Ayaan: Is your father going to marry my mom? Is he going to leave you people and come and stay with us?

Ayaan is not at all surprised with this question, since Vikram had already updated him about his and Purvi's relation on the way. So, he replies: That is not possible Ananya. Our parents can remain good friends, and can take care of each other, and be there for each other at all times - good or bad. Vikram interferes, wanting to clarify once and for all. Very politely, he says to Ananya: Ananya, it's true that your mom and I have known each other since college days, and we did want to marry each other; but that was then. Now, I have a family, and so does your mom. We cannot just leave our families and run away from our responsibilities just because we have met again. Even your grandparents are not going to approve of our relationship. They did not then, they will not now.

Vikram assures Ananya that they all can be like one big happy family but without formalities and commitments such as marriage.

Marriage was not to be. not then, not now.

Purvi is satisfied and happy with what Vikram said to Ananya. Deep inside, even she knew that marriage was not possible at this stage of life. She was 41, separated from her husband for the last 12 years. Separated… not divorced. And this was a second chance life was giving her to remain friends with Vikram. To be with him. She knew he will be there for her when no one else will. Purvi now knows that Vikram is committed to his family, and she also knows that he will be committed to her - not as a husband, but as a very good and very close friend.

Purvi knew that Ananya was a kid, and was taking Vikram seriously, as if wanting him to be her daddy. But she thought that with time, Ananya will understand that it was not possible.

By 8:30 pm, the coffee and the conversation are almost over. Ananya has got her answers. Ayaan is satisfied by what his father has said to Ananya. He loves his father a lot and knows very well that his father will not do anything to hurt anybody in any manner and will not make promises that he cannot fulfil. They end the meeting on a happy note. Purvi hugs Ayaan, Ayaan hugs Ananya, they say bye to each other, and leave.

INTROSPECTION

Vikram and Purvi are in regular touch. They call and message each other all the time. Love is all it is.

It has been four days since they met in the mall, and Vikram has been thinking of meeting Purvi again before her parents return from South Africa, which is the day after tomorrow. The meeting with Ananya and Purvi has left Vikram with some thoughts and questions - thoughts that have been troubling him since and questions that can only be answered by Purvi herself. Lately, he has been introspecting...has it been right of him to bring back Purvi in his life? He loved her, and that was something he could not change. He knows he had missed her all these years, but that was it. However, what he was doing now, was it love or sympathy? Or both? He was confused.

The questions troubling him were what was Purvi expecting from him? Was she still in love with him after all these years and after what all had happened in her life? Did she really want to be with him? And, what would this relation be? Friends? Friends about whom neither he nor she can tell anyone? Secondly... what was Ananya expecting from him? The kid had asked his son(Ayaan) if his father was going to leave them (his family) and stay with them (Purvi's family).

Vikram knows life is tough for Purvi. It is not easy to manage things alone, there has to be someone you can depend upon mentally, physically, and financially. He knows the kids miss their father.

Maybe that is why Ananya asked Ayaan that kiddish question of him (Vikram) marrying her mother.

Vikram is also thinking about Purvi's husband. What kind of a man can leave his beautiful wife and loveable kids and live with his own mother? He thinks about asking Purvi to go back to her husband. If not for herself, then maybe for the kids' sake. A patch-up might be possible. So, he calls Purvi and asks if they can meet before her parents return. She says they can meet tomorrow evening as it is a Sunday, her holiday, and she would be able to finish all her work by the afternoon. So, the time is fixed and Vikram has to pick Purvi up from her house.

Vikram reaches Purvi's place at dot 6:00 in the evening. He is very punctual about time. He gives a missed call on her mobile to signal that he has reached and is waiting outside. She comes out of the house and sits in the car. Vikram wants to spend the evening at some quiet and peaceful place where he can sit and talk to Purvi (the issues are such), without his attention being diverted by people or by food. So, he takes her to a five-star hotel which is not too far and they go to one of its best restaurants which serves beer and snacks at all times (since, it's too early for dinner). They reach there at 6:20 pm. There's a counter at the entrance of the restaurant, where a young stewardess is stationed to guide the guests and note down their details. The stewardess is smilingly asking Vikram his details, when suddenly Purvi is irritated by something (God knows what) and calls her a 'bitch' in a very hushed tone. Vikram is a bit taken aback. He looks at Purvi with disapproval. He asks Purvi why she used that derogatory word. She replies, that she did not like the way the stewardess looked at him.

Vikram should have discussed with Purvi, why she was irritated and why did she use a cuss word for an unknown woman, but he did not want to waste time on this lame issue. Of course, how was he to know then that a cuss word would later become the root cause of a fight so ugly, that he would barely survive it? Anyway, at that point, he lets it go because he does not want to spoil his or her mood. He does not want to spoil the evening. He was here for a very important discussion. So, he avoids getting into an unwanted situation. There are no guests in the restaurant at this time and they sit at a table in a corner and order beer and some snacks.

Purvi has a very innocent and pretty face. One look at her and anybody will either sympathise with her or will fall in love with her (of course, she is sexy). Vikram keeps looking at her, wondering where to start from. After some time, Purvi starts the conversation.

Purvi: How is Ayaan? It was wonderful meeting him that day. He's so charming.

Vikram: Ayaan's good, and yes, he is charming, thank you. Ananya is also pretty, though she doesn't look like you.

The waiter gets the beer bottles and snacks. Purvi helps in serving the snacks and the focus shifts from the kids ....

Purvi: Mom and dad are coming back tomorrow. They had a wonderful time in South Africa.

Vikram: That's nice ....so you will be busier from tomorrow ... Anyways ...let's talk about ourselves. We have to catch-up on a lot of things. I have missed you all these years. 23 years is a long time. You just stopped talking, meeting, got married and disappeared. We could have remained friends ....

Ek umr guzaari tere bina, tu saath toh thee per saath nahin ....

Jiye is kadar tere bina, ki baat toh thee per baat nahin ....

Aankhon mein tere bina, neend toh thee per khwaab nahin....

Dil mein tere bina kayi, sawaal toh the per jawaab nahin ....

Purvi is not amused...she doesn't like Vikram's poetry and smirks: Your poetry does not have the same punch as earlier.

Vikram nods, and gets back to the subject ....so tell me, what happened after we stopped talking and meeting?

Purvi looks at Vikram and smiles. This was one topic she wanted to avoid. Last time they had gone for lunch, she had told Vikram that he was the reason for all the nuisance in her life, and that it was his fault that they did not get married. And now ... he was again starting the same topic. She didn't want to answer; so instead she asked Vikram, what had his life been like after the break-up.

Vikram knew this was coming. He knows her too well. So, to make her comfortable he starts telling his side of the story: After the breakup, life was not easy. The more I tried to forget you, the more I thought about you. You were my first crush and the last! There was not a month in these 23 years, when I did not think about you. I always used to wonder how you were doing in life, who did you get married to, were your in-laws very rich, was your husband very handsome, how many kids did you have, where did you live, will we ever meet again, will we ever talk, will I ever get to know what happened with your life. So many questions used to go on constantly in my mind. So yes, in short, I used to think a lot about you ...and maybe the Gods listened my prayers, and said okay, we will give you one chance. They have really been very kind to me. As for other things in life, well, after college, I started my business. As you know, we were a middle-class family, and didn't have enough money to start something big. So, I had to work very hard to succeed. In some time, the business started doing well, and I started making good money. Then, my parents started looking for a match for me within the family, since they both had a huge circle of relatives who were eager to help. Anjali was the daughter of a second cousin of my father. I got married...and now we have two kids, one of them who you met last week. That's just about it. This has been my story so far.

In between, the waiter comes and fills up the empty glasses of beer.

Vikram then tells Purvi all about his business, his family, his friends and everything that he can tell in the shortest of time because, he wanted to hear her version. He was here to hear her, mainly.

Purvi is looking relaxed. Vikram smiles. He can see the tension easing from her face. So, he asks her: What about you? How was your life after college?

Purvi is a very confident woman with a very strong personality but she has to be in her comfort zone to tell her story, and now she seemed at ease. Without delay and without any hesitation, she speaks: After our break-up, I used to fight about you a lot at home with mom and dad. They asked me to complete my education and said that you will also settle in business by then. So, when the right time comes, they will go and talk to your parents. Till then, I was told, not to talk to you or meet you. Even the landline phone was monitored all the time. Mom-dad made sure I didn't talk to you.

Vikram interferes in between: Your dad had come to meet my dad, a year after our break-up. What did they tell you about that? Your cousin Vivek had also accompanied your dad. (Vivek was Purvi's cousin. He had been adopted by her parents, because they had three daughters and no son).

Purvi looks clueless. Vikram continues: They had some conversation. It must not have been cordial, because my dad was very upset after the meeting. He did not share the details of the meeting with me; just asked me to forget about you.

Purvi: I don't remember much about what had happened then; just that my father was going to your place and they were going to talk about our marriage. I was not told what had happened there. But soon after that, they started looking for a match for me. Then one day, they said they had finalized a boy for me. He was mom's cousin's son. They lived in a bungalow in Civil Lines and had an electronics' shop in Chandni Chowk. The next year, I got married ....

Again, Vikram interrupts to ask: What's his name?

Purvi replies: Ramit. So, after I got married, it was fine for some time, and then the troubles started. A few months later, I was pregnant and Ramit was on a business trip to Bangalore. One of our relatives (an aunt who also lived in Bangalore and at whose place Ramit had stayed a few times) called and said that she had seen Ramit with another woman. She was sure it was some prostitute with him as she had seen different women with him earlier too.

I was devastated, I cried a lot that night, all alone in my room and five months pregnant. Who could I tell or share what that aunty had told me about Ramit? Ours was a joint family, with my father in-law's elder brother's family also staying in the same house on the first floor. They wanted to sell the property, divide the money, and go their separate ways. Businesses of both the families were not running well. My mother in-law was very snobbish and bossy. She used to give me a tough time, always saying something or the other, taunting for something or the other. Often, she would ask me to get money from my parents. She would always say, your parents are so rich and should support us in these bad times. Even after knowing about my husband's philandering ways, and my in-laws torturing me over money issues, I never used to say anything to anybody. Deep inside, I knew my life had been ruined and nothing could be done about that. Once, when I was seven months pregnant, Ramit asked me to get Rs. 10 lakhs from my parents as they had to clear some company's balance payments or the business would get shut down. I went to my parents' house and asked daddy for money (not knowing that this was just the beginning of extortion by my in-laws). He gave the money readily, not asking any questions. He just wanted me to be happy.

I gave the money to Ramit in the presence of my in-laws. Both my in-laws were delighted. They understood, I was a goose that lay the golden eggs. They knew they had a daughter in-law who will fulfil all their demands. They knew that daddy was a rich man ....

A month and a half later when Ananya was due any moment, my in-laws again asked me to get some money from daddy. I refused because I had just borrowed a huge sum from him and moreover, I didn't want to trouble him so soon again. We had an argument and Ramit beat me up. I bled from my left ear and my lips and cheeks were all swollen ....

Vikram points at her bit broken third upper tooth on the left side and she acknowledges, it was from that incident only.

She continues: I still refused to ask my parents for money. Those days were really tense; each day would feel like a year. A week later, Ananya was born. Mom and dad came to see us. They gave another Rs. 5 lakhs as a token of love and blessings. They didn't even mention about the Rs. 10 lakhs I had borrowed before. The fights and arguments stopped for a few months, because I was busy with Ananya, and the in-laws had got their hands on the Rs. 5 lakhs I had received from mom-dad; but still, the tension remained. I could feel it all the time.

The waiter comes and asks if they would have some more beer or snacks. Purvi asks him to get two more bottles and some chicken tikka. Vikram was listening very attentively; her story was intriguing. This was Purvi's journey from being an absolutely beautiful and sexy girl to a separated wife with two kids. He was wondering, if she had married him (Vikram), what life would have been like for both of them? The mistake that Purvi's father made by choosing Ramit for her, why didn't he make that mistake with him?

Duniya bahut dekhi humne, fir bhi kam dekhi gaafil....

Khushiyaan cheen cheen kar yeh, badle mein gham degi gaafil ....

Purvi continues: After a year or so, the arguments, the fights, the torture by Ramit, all started again. He used to beat me, abuse me, ask me to get money from my parents. The house was put on the market for sale, the shop was shut and sold off. Where the money from the sale went, nobody knows. My father in-law and his brother were always fighting. It was like a madhouse! Everybody always fighting with everybody.

Here Purvi pauses to sigh and then says. What a family I was married into!

Then she continues: On the other hand, my dad was keen on winding up his business. For him, we three daughters were all settled, and he didn't want to work forever. He wanted to lead a peaceful, retired, happy life. So, he sold off his two factories. Actually, Ajay jijaji – Seema's husband - was not in favour of the factories being sold, so he asked daddy to give one to him, since the factories were minting money at that point of time; but daddy declined. Due to that, Ajay jijaji is angry with daddy to this day. Daddy sold the factories and then also sold the two upper floors of the house. He got rid of all the liabilities and put all the money in the bank. Mom and dad then decided to give Rs. 25 lakh each to us three daughters. They gave Anita and Seema their share. I refused to take the money and said I will take it when needed. My in-laws were too greedy and I had already given them Rs. 15 lakhs.

Vikram interrupts again: What happened to Vivek, that cousin of yours?

Purvi: He was mom's sister's son. Mom-dad had adopted him because we didn't have a brother. They gave him good education, made him a partner in one of the factories, gave him a flat to live in, got him married. His marriage ceremony had been a five-star affair. But then, he got too ambitious. He thought daddy was going to give him his factories, which he could not and finally did not. He had a huge argument and then, a fight with daddy. After that he left for Canada with his wife. After some time, he got divorced and then one day, he committed suicide.

Vikram was sorry to hear Vivek's story. He was a fine guy (at least, he had tried to be). Vikram had met him once, when Vivek had called and asked him to meet, after coming to know about his and Purvi's affair. In the beginning of the conversation, he had tried to threaten and intimidate Vikram indirectly, telling him about his mafia connections. But once they got talking, he knew Vikram was not a man to be threatened. He was polite afterwards.

Vikram asks Purvi to excuse him for a minute and goes to the washroom. All through, he keeps thinking about all the twists and turns of time. Vivek is no more (got only the promises perhaps), Ajay jijaji is not happy (he didn't get the factory), Purvi is not happy (her marriage went bad). What has become of the world and who was responsible for all this? Maybe the Gods or maybe they themselves. Or perhaps, it was their Karma.

Vikram comes back and Purvi goes to the washroom.

She comes back and sits with a smile. Vikram asks her to continue.

Purvi: Time was passing and my relations with my in-laws were getting worse day by day. Ramit used to beat me every now and then. Once he was drunk and asked me to call daddy to demand money. I refused. He got violent and beat me up. He called daddy and made him listen to my cries for help over the phone. Ananya was growing up and she used to see Ramit beating me up. She used to cry whenever Ramit would beat me. A few weeks later, I gave in to the pressure for my and Ananya's sake. Shamefully, I asked daddy for another Rs. 8 lakh and gave it to my in-laws. A few months later the house was sold and the money was divided between my father-in-law and his elder brother. We shifted to a small rented house for some time. This house was too small for the five of us, so after a while, my in-laws asked me and Ramit to move out with Ananya to another rented place till the time they bought a house of their own. So, I along with Ananya and Ramit, shifted to a one-bedroom, third floor house in Model Town. Ramit was good for nothing; he had nothing to do except drinking and fighting with me. Financially, we were still dependent on whatever money the in-laws gave us for rent and expenses. Then I got pregnant again.

Vikram was aghast! How could she have sex and then get pregnant by a man who was so brutal to her? By someone who screwed her life, who screwed her parents' life and who wanted her money and not her? how could she do the act with him?

But he did not say anything. He wanted to hear the complete story and he did not want to stop the flow.

Purvi: In September 2000, Chhotu, my son was born. No one from my in-law's family came to bless us. Mom-dad visited and were happy. They thought that having a son in the family might change my in-laws and Ramit's behaviour. They were even thinking of supporting us financially. After a few months, Ramit said he was going out of station with my father-in-law for some business, and will be back in 3-4 days. But a fortnight passed and yet, he didn't turn up. I was worried. The landlord was asking for rent, Ananya's pre-school fee was due, there was no grocery in the kitchen, there was hardly anything to eat and I had very little money. I took a rickshaw with Chhotu in my arms and Ananya sitting beside me, and went to my in-laws rented house. I repeatedly knocked on the door and rang the bell, but no one opened the door. I was crying. My tears flowed nonstop. (Even as she recounts those terrible times, Purvi's eyes start watering up. Vikram holds her hand to comfort her.)

Jo hote hum saath, toh gham naa hota ....

Pyaar apna tujhse, kabhi kam naa hota ....

bitha ker rakhte, tujhe palkon pe hamesha ....

Tere siva duniya mein, koi hum-dum naa hota ....

Purvi (almost in tears): I took an auto-rickshaw and came back to mom-dad.

Vikram offers her a glass of water but she takes a sip from her beer glass instead. Then she smiles and says: I'm happy to be with you.

Vikram asks her: Do you want to order any food?

Purvi replies: No thanks, I'm enjoying my beer and snacks.

Then, she continues with her story: After coming back, I told the entire story to mom and dad. They felt sorry for me and said I should not worry about anything. They assured me of sorting out all the problems. The next day, daddy called a few relatives and tried to locate Ramit. One of the relatives told daddy that Ramit was staying with his parents and had not gone for any business tour. He also told daddy that when I (Purvi) had gone to my in-laws place along with the two kids, the three of them (Ramit and his mom dad) were at home only. They had not opened the door because they did not want her (Purvi) in their life no more. Daddy was furious but he had got his answers and he knew that things would never be right again. So, after a few days, he called Mr Bhatia (a friend and a lawyer practicing in high court) and sought his advice. Mr Bhatia advised me not to divorce Ramit, for if I divorced him, he would be free of all the obligations and will be free to marry again. Mr Bhatia also said that, a man who has destroyed your life should not be set free. Moreover, he suggested that we should not deny the kids their legal rights. They will be the heirs to what all Ramit has (Ramit's father is no more and they have a kothi in Noida now). Ramit is into interior designing, is gay, and lives with his mom and boyfriend. So, the family decided not to file for divorce, and I and the kids started staying with mom-dad.

It's already 9:20 pm and Vikram asks Purvi if she would like to have dinner. She says she's full with the beer and snacks and would rather just go home (she looks a bit tipsy). Vikram pays the bill and they leave, holding hands. Vikram drives her home and she asks him to come inside. She says the kids had gone to their dadi's (grandmother) house and would be coming late.

Vikram parks the car across the road in front of Purvi's house. Purvi unlocks the main door, switches the lights on, and leads him to the living room. They sit on the sofa; she holds his hand and smiles.

(Purvi has the most wonderful smile in the world after Sharmila Tagore)

Purvi asks Vikram if he would like to have some coffee or something; he refuses. Vikram is still thinking about Ramit. He wants to ask Purvi about reconciliation, about her going back to Ramit; but, without spoiling her mood. After all, she is looking so happy. So, very cautiously he ventures: The kids are cordial with their dadi and papa, is it? Do you also meet them?

Purvi: Kids are okay with their dad and dadi. I also go there sometimes, just for formality's sake. If there's some function or celebration, I go, but otherwise I don't like going there.

Vikram: You never thought of going back to Ramit? I mean, you guys are not divorced, you have two kids and now he has a house and a business of his own.

Purvi: My mother-in-law is a very cunning woman. She never felt sorry for what she did to me. She still loves money, she still likes to play games, she still blames me for everything (that I could have come back after some time, time heals all wounds, that I should take care of her and Ramit, after all they are my family... blah, blah, blah). Huh! Family! What family? Ramit is gay. He lives with his boyfriend in the same house and my mother-in-law knows that; and you are asking me if I have ever thought of going back? I don't want to go back. Ever. What I have gone through, all that torture ...physical abuse, emotional abuse, financial abuse... only I know. They are monsters.

Purvi has tears in her eyes. She is holding Vikram's hand tightly, as if telling him: Don't leave me this time.

Vikram looks her in the eyes, as if telling her: Not this time dearie, not this time.

Waqt nahin tha saath, aur dikkat bahut thee ....

thama na kisi ne haath, per himmat bahut thee ....

Milaya us khuda ne, bichhde huon ko gaafil ....

Maani meri yeh baat, ki tujhse mohabbat bahut thee....

Vikram takes Purvi in his arms and gives her a tight hug. They hold each other tightly, embracing each other. They can feel each other's breath. Her left cheek is touching Vikram's left cheek, her chest - Vikram's chest. She is in tears and Vikram can feel them on his cheek. He doesn't move. She doesn't move. Sitting on the sofa, they embrace each other so tightly that it seems they are one soul and one body. They had never embraced each other before, and now, the gods had given them that one chance they both desired. It was a wonderful feeling, a feeling better than having sex. They sit like that for at least half an hour embracing each other, gazing into each other's eyes, smiling, feeling each other, knowing that they are there for each other.

Vikram spends some time with her and then leaves, her children were supposed to be back anytime.

Vikram and Purvi still love and care for each other and have expressed their feelings to each other openly. They have committed to be best friends for life, come what may. Committed to be there for each other in all circumstances. She doesn't want to go back to her husband (it's been twelve years since she left him) and she also accepts Vikram's marital status. They both promise to keep their relation uncomplicated, hassle free, not disturbing each other's peaceful lives (since they both have families) and no promises of marriage (she is separated and not divorced. He will not divorce Anjali).

THE OVER-INDULGED

Purvi's parents are back from South Africa and she gets busy with school, home, and family. Vikram and Purvi don't meet for the next couple of days. They just talk and message on the phone.

One day, Purvi calls Vikram and asks: Can you accompany Ananya for her college admissions tomorrow? I want you to go with her just in case some help is needed. I have school, and it is not possible for me to take a leave and go with her. I'll be grateful if you can pick Ananya, take her to college, pay the fees, and drop her back.

Vikram: No worries at all. It's okay. What time should I pick her up, and which college do we have to go to?

Purvi: Pick her at 10:00 in the morning and she will tell you the details.

Next day, Vikram picks up Ananya from her house.

Ananya is a 17-year-old teenager, just out of a reputed co-ed, South Delhi school. Now, this South Delhi school has its own story. While the students studying there call it a reputed school, it is famous for its spoilt boys and girls from rich and influential families. It does have some studious and topper students too, but the overall reputation is of boys and girls having affairs from very young ages, mass-bunking from school, guys and girls smoking and drinking, after school parties, late night parties ...so on and so forth.

Ananya is a masterpiece. A smart, modern teenage girl, full of over-confidence. She loves to show off. Loves to talk loudly in English so that she can be heard. Loves to wear all kinds of jazzy &

revealing clothes (even her brother Chhotu objects to her wearing such clothes). Loves to go out with friends (boyfriends), loves to get drunk, loves to puke, loves to argue, loves to scream, loves to abuse (she doesn't even spare her mom), loves to use Hindi cuss words…et al. A complete attention-seeking masterpiece, Purvi says Ananya has been troubling her since she was in class eight. She says, she doesn't trust Ananya at all and that, Ananya has all the traits of her father including his habit of compulsive lying. The girl is always interested in boys and has many boyfriends.

Vikram is not interested in the girl's life or her story. He is there only to help Purvi. He knows he is not Ananya's father and he cannot be one; but because of Purvi, he will sometimes have to look after her kids too. He will have to be there for them too. On face value, Ananya looks very innocent, polite, and decent (she projects herself this way to outsiders: smart girl).

Vikram takes Ananya to the college she is seeking admission in, not talking much on the way. Ananya completes all the formalities and they leave for home.

On the way Ananya says to Vikram: Uncle, I wanted to study in a co-ed college, but mom didn't allow me to.

Vikram: Ananya, it doesn't matter what college you go to, beta. You have a wonderful family; you have friends from school and colony. Just concentrate on your studies and career. Your mom has gone through a lot in life. Make her proud. And just in case, you need my help ever, for anything, I will be there for you.

He treats Ananya like his daughter and advises her just like he would have advised Ayaan or Aryan. On the way, he messages Purvi that the college admission is secured and he is dropping Ananya home. They reach her house; Ananya says thanks and goes inside the house. Vikram thinks she is a sweet child. What he doesn't know is that, the girl he was just guiding, and promising to be there for her at all times (as a father figure), will one day teach him the biggest lesson of his life. That no one in this world is to be trusted, if not me by my mother, then not my mother by you.

A few days later, it is Ananya's eighteenth birthday and she wants to celebrate it in a big way. She wants to invite all her school, colony and college friends. Purvi calls Vikram and asks him to book some good place for the celebration. Vikram happily obliges. He books a good place and makes fancy arrangements for the party, as if Ananya was his own daughter. The party is a hit and everybody has a great time.

Only .... Vikram is not invited .... and he doesn't mind. He goes and pays the bill after the party is over and everybody has gone home.

A few weeks later, Ananya calls Vikram and asks for his help in getting permission from Purvi, for going to a late-night party. Vikram calls Purvi and requests her to allow Ananya to go. Ananya goes to the party, gets drunk, and throws up. Ananya's friends call Purvi and ask her to pick her up. At around 12 in the night, Purvi goes with Chhotu, picks Ananya from the pub, and takes her home. Mother and daughter fight and abuse each other all the way back home.

This is just the beginning of Ananya's party tales. Every second month, without fail, the mother-daughter duo fight over Ananya's partying ways; and Vikram makes sure, he is not to be involved ... he is there to help, not to take the blames.

THE FATHER

The next time Vikram comes to meet Purvi, they are sitting in the car and talking. The car is parked outside house no. 116. After a while, two policemen who are on patrol duty arrive and stop their bike just next to their car. The one riding the bike says: Roll down your window. Vikram rolls down the window glass and looks at him, as if asking what his problem was. but before Vikram can say anything, the constable sarcastically says: Be mindful of your age, and again, before Vikram can reply, he zooms off. Vikram is upset and looks at Purvi. She is also upset. Can't two 40+ people just sit in the car and talk? Just talk. They were not indulging in any activity of any other sort. Not even holding hands. Just sitting plainly and talking, like any husband-wife will do. This was a bit weird… anybody can come and say anything to you and you can't even object or defend yourself. Vikram asks Purvi to go home, but she doesn't want to go. Vikram explains to her that it is not right to sit in the car and talk, as any known person can see them and create a problem for them both. Her daddy also comes for evening walks; what if he sees them together some day? So, they decide that they will drive around whenever they meet, and meet only late evenings, when it is a bit dark and the possibility of anyone recognising them is low. Purvi says that she misses him too much and wants to meet him more often and for longer durations.

Vikram then says that he has an idea, that whenever he has to go for business meetings, he will always take her along. That way they would be able to meet more often.

Few days later, he and Purvi go to attend such a meeting (it is a late-evening meeting) where another business associate Mr. Gupta, who knows Vikram and his family very well, meets them accidentally. On seeing Vikram with another woman and not his wife, he gets curious. He deliberately comes to meet Vikram, says hello to him and then enquires about the woman accompanying him. Vikram says to him that she is a first cousin and excuses himself and leaves the place with Purvi.

On the way, Purvi says: It was none of Mr Gupta's business to enquire about me.

Vikram replies: People are less interested in their own lives and more so in others.

Khaali hai mann, khaali hai khayal ....

Fir bhi woh, karte hain sawaal ....

Jinko nahin samajh zamaane ki ...

Har baat pe woh, karte hain bawaal ...

Vikram is not happy about this incident. He says: Gupta is not a man to be trusted. He is a gossip monger. He might make up stories and tell other business friends. I don't want unnecessary attention, rumours, or badmouthing about you and me.

Purvi: What can we do now? What has happened has happened. We cannot change that. But let's be careful from now on.

Vikram: We cannot meet so often and so openly, Purvi. That day, it was the policeman, today it is Gupta, tomorrow it can be someone known to you or some other acquaintance of mine. That will not be good for either of us. We will have to find some other way of meeting.

Vikram is about to drop Purvi to her house and they are on the road leading to her house when Purvi sees her father standing outside the house, perhaps waiting for her. She says to Vikram: Daddy is waiting outside. Maybe because I'm late. You stop the car at 114, drop me and just go. Don't wait to say bye. Just go. Vikram slows down the car, sees Purvi's father - Mr Nand Kishore - stops the car at 114, drops Purvi, again looks back at Mr Nand Kishore and drives off very slowly, still looking at him in the rear-view mirror. Vikram can't believe what he has just seen. This man is not even a shadow of what he looked like in the 1990s. That time, he had the personality of a rich, spoilt by money kind of a man, full of ego and with a negative attitude for anybody he didn't like. When he had seen Vikram for the first time in 1992, he had looked at Vikram in a very insulting way, straightaway rejecting him as if he had come prepared to reject him.

Vikram was now seeing Mr Nand Kishore after exactly 21 years. He had last seen him in 1992, when Mr Nand Kishore had come to his house to meet his dad. He remembered that face very well for all these years. The face of the man who had destroyed Vikram emotionally. The trauma he had left in Vikram's mind was uncurable. First, he had threatened Vikram's dad and then made a mockery of Vikram himself, just because they were financially not sound at that point of time. Mr Nand Kishore was a wealthy man. How could he bear his daughter falling in love with a man who lived in a two-bedroom house with his family? So, he married her into a family that too lived in a bungalow, not knowing that they were fake and frauds and were on the verge of bankruptcy.

Now, this old man, 74 years old, standing in front of his house, looks very weak, very fragile, very lonely. The look on his face tells that he has accepted the truths of his life and maybe the faults too. He knows that he has spoilt his daughter's life unknowingly and Vikram's too, knowingly.

Shakhs badal jaate hain, shakhsiyat badal jaati hai, waqt ke saath ....

Jo waqt na de saath, toh milkiyat badal jaati hai, waqt ke saath ....

SOME PLACE ELSE

Vikram and Purvi decide that they won't meet during day time. It will only be late evenings (when it is a bit dark) at around 7:30 -8:00. They fix a place (from where Vikram will pick her from now onwards), which is near to her house, but because it is a busy main road with regular flow of heavy traffic, nobody will bother about who is going where and who is coming from where. Next time, Purvi tells at home that she is going to a friend's house and would be coming only after dinner (dinner for family and other household work has already been taken care of). The moment she steps out of the house, her dad comes after her, as if suspicious of where she is going and with whom. She asks him to go back in and starts walking towards the designated place. She calls Vikram and asks him where he is. Vikram says he is already there at the designated spot, waiting for her.

Purvi comes and sits in the car and they drive off. She says she is sorry for keeping him waiting. He smiles at her. She holds his hand and rests her head on his shoulder. Vikram likes it when she shows such affection to him. He had missed this love all these years when they were not together. Vikram is thinking and is confused as to where to take her - a place which is safe and where nobody can see them.

They are just driving around when Vikram sees a lot of upmarket guest houses on the main road. He has an idea. They can book a room in a five-star hotel or a guest house away from public eye for an hour or two, sit, talk, eat and go back home with nobody seeing them. He discusses this idea with Purvi and she instantly agrees.

They decide to go to a place which is a bit far from both their houses. After driving a few kilometres, they stop at a guest house which looks upscale, park the car, go to the reception and ask for a room. The receptionist updates them about the room rent (Rs. 4000), the facilities provided, and asks for an ID for registering their name in their database. Vikram gives his driving licence as ID proof, pays Rs. 4000 upfront and takes the keys to room no. 215 on the first floor. He then calls room service and asks for two cups of coffee and two chicken sandwiches. Vikram and Purvi sit on the sofa facing each other and start talking. The doorbell rings. A boy comes in and keeps the coffee and sandwiches on the table and leaves. They resume talking; the topic of their conversation is their future together.

Vikram says that he loves her a lot and would not like to lose her, as he had lost her before. He says it was the worst thing to happen in his life and he had never been able to get over it.

Purvi says she loves him too and understands him. She says that she herself had gone through the trauma of losing him and that she would never force him for anything. It is the love between the two that mattered, nothing else.

Vikram says it won't be possible for him to leave his kids and wife and marry her. He won't do to his family what Ramit had done to Purvi and her kids.

Purvi says she knows that it is not possible. She says she still wants to be in a relationship with him, that their love is above all commitments. They didn't need to marry or divorce to be together.

Khoya tha kabhi, pa liya hai aaj gaafil ...

Kal tak the, teri mohabbat ke mohtaj gaafil ....

Shukr hai khuda ka, milaya tujhse mujhko ...

Jo Kal the begaane, aaj hain humraaj gaafil ....

They stay in the room for almost two hours and leave around 10:00 pm. Purvi is very happy to be with him, and Vikram loves to see her smile. He drops her and goes back home …happy and smiling.

The guest house turns out to be a good idea. It is posh, comfortable, convenient, secure, secret, and sacred for Vikram and Purvi. It becomes a second home for them. They go there twice, and sometimes even thrice a week. He picks her late evenings and drops her only when she feels like going home. Vikram pampers her with love; she pampers him with more love in return. Money (room rent, snacks, drinks, dinner) is not important; their happiness is important. Purvi tries to keep an account of how much money Vikram is spending and sometimes asks him to be less extravagant. But Vikram has no control over his spending habits. She was supposed to be his wife and he was supposed to take good care of her. So, what if they didn't marry for whatever reasons? He could still make her happy….

After a few visits, all the staff at the guest house start knowing them well, and sometimes when the owner is around, even he greets them. Anybody could take Vikram and Purvi for husband and wife. They looked so good together. A couple in their 40s cannot be doubted for having an illegitimate relationship. They don't even look like they are having an extra-marital affair. Their chemistry is such that once Chhotu, Purvi's son, sees them together (when Vikram comes to drop her) he tells her that they looked like husband and wife. Never had he seen his mother so happy and glowing in his thirteen years.

In between, Purvi and Ananya have been fighting and arguing very frequently. The reasons for the fights are Ananya's lies, her meetings with boyfriends, and her going to late night parties. Every now and then, she wants permission and money. A few times, she calls up Vikram and asks him to tell mom to permit her, which Vikram does. He himself goes to pick Ananya from the parties late in the night and drop her home - sometimes with Purvi, sometimes alone. Each time the mother-daughter duo fight, Vikram always stands with Purvi (without Ananya knowing) for mental support. The issues are always resolved after Purvi talks to Vikram. With time, they start talking and behaving like husband-wife, seeking each other's advice for every matter ...big or small. Every few days, Purvi complains to Vikram about Ananya's behaviour and he always advises her to be gentle with the girl. He says, Ananya is in transformation; she is now in college, wants more freedom, wants to enjoy life, wants to say more, wants to be heard more, wants to be acknowledged as a grownup sensible kid you don't have to guide anymore. So, he asks Purvi to be gentle and patient with Ananya.

Once she goes to party at a pub near Vikram's house, and Purvi comes to pick her at around 12 in the night with Chhotu. Ananya is drunk and refuses to leave the party. Purvi calls Vikram and asks him to accompany her to the party venue. Vikram brings Ayaan along and sends Ayaan inside the pub to call Ananya. Ananya is drunk and furious. She comes and starts hurling abuses at Purvi. Ananya is calling Purvi a bitch, an asshole, in the middle of the road with people looking at them. Vikram and Ayaan are stunned to see her behaving in this manner. Purvi tells Vikram to not be surprised; this is what Ananya does every time she goes to a party. Every time she gets drunk, and every time she abuses, if asked to leave party earlier than she desires. Vikram and Ayaan ask Ananya to sit in their car and drive her home. The entire way she keeps complaining to Vikram about her mom and Vikram keeps asking her to cool down. He assures Ananya that he will talk to Purvi and sort the matter out.

Can the matters be sorted? Not at all. Ananya is not the type to mend her ways and Purvi is not the sorry feeling types. Both have their own egos, and Vikram is an outsider, who will be grinded, like in a mixer grinder, by both of them, in years to come.

THE SPOILER

Purvi has a friend, Monisha. They used to teach in the same school at one point of time and have been friends for last ten years. This woman is a replica of Komolika from the telly-soap KASAUTI ZINDAGI KI. The only difference is that Komolika always conspires for money and power whereas Monisha conspires for artificial happiness and sex. She is not happy and sexually satisfied with her husband. The guy is employed with a MNC and is working round the clock, whereas she is always scheming on how to get men from Facebook to her bedroom in the absence of her patni-vrata (devout) husband. Whenever he goes on an official tour or even to regular office, Monisha experiments and experiences all kinds of Kamasutra actions and positions with men who she lures for free enjoyment and entertainment. Six months was the maximum given time to a gigolo.

Monisha is sort of a mentor to Purvi; a free sex consultant like they have in Daryaganj (Old Delhi)). She would guide Purvi and ill-advise her on how to be confident, how to pursue, and how to deal with men. She would freely tell Purvi how to seduce a man (or men). Monisha is an encyclopaedia on sexual desires and knows how to make men fall on their knees and beg for sex. She knows in detail what is going on in between Purvi and Vikram. Only, Vikram doesn't know that Monisha knew so much about them or that, she is the one guiding Purvi. Had he known, he would have maintained a distance from both of them. And, by the time he got to know...it was too late.

In the month of October, during the Durga puja days, Purvi asks Vikram to accompany her to a puja pandal. She says this pandal has been organised by her best friend Monisha, and that she has told Monisha about him and Monisha was very excited to meet him. Purvi says that Monisha wanted to see Vikram as she had told her their story and she couldn't believe that a man can love a woman for these many years. Vikram is hesitant; he doesn't want to acquaint anyone; he doesn't want anyone to know his story. But he cannot say no to Purvi, and she is also not ready to take a no for an answer. So, Vikram picks Purvi and they go together to meet Monisha.

They reach there and look for Monisha. Monisha sees them and waves her hand. Purvi introduces Vikram to Monisha. Vikram is a lost man who is not interested in women, doesn't matter how beautiful or sexy they are. Monisha is wearing a white saree with red border in a typical Bengali style with an extra-large size, red coloured bindi on her forehead, which is looking weird and not suiting her already not-so-good personality. Vikram is already not interested in meeting her as he thought this meeting was arranged to get a stamp of approval from Monisha to see whether he was good enough for Purvi, looks-wise and personality-wise.

He is a man who has seen it all and knows it all, and he has a gut-feeling that this woman is not right for their relationship. But he cannot object to their accord because Monisha's equation with Purvi is stronger than his with Purvi. He knows that he will have to tolerate Purvi's relationship with Monisha (like accepting an undesirable package of 'buy one get one free'). Monisha shakes hands with Vikram, says hello and looks at him excitedly. Vikram is not excited to meet her, nor does he want to stay at this place for long. He doesn't like Monisha at first sight. He is not impressed with her in any way, and just says hello coolly. Moreover, he is uncomfortable whenever he is at a public place with Purvi. It is like, somebody known always comes out of the blue to meet him when he is with Purvi. So, he wants to avoid being seen at public places with her. It can cause discomfort and embarrassment to her and to him.

So, after a while, Vikram asks Purvi whether they should go home. Purvi, who has been chatting with Monisha all this while, asks him to wait for a few more minutes and then after completing her conversation with Monisha, says bye to her. Monisha says bye to her and to Vikram, and they leave. Vikram is very uncomfortable with what Purvi has said to Monisha about them both (the woman knows the entire story of him meeting her – from college days till now). He is bothered by the fact that Purvi is making personal relations, public. Their reunion was not meant to be shared with anybody, no matter who it was or how close she was with that person. You are not supposed to be sharing the details of your moments of intimacy with a third person, that is the code of love and Purvi was breaking the protocol. But, Vikram doesn't say anything; he chooses to remain silent on this matter.

It is a bit late in the evening and Vikram has not had anything since lunch. They go to a takeaway joint and order chicken and paneer rolls. The waiter who serves them says hello to Vikram. This man has served Vikram many times when he has come with his family. Now he is giving Vikram a weird look, seeing him with Purvi. To Vikram, it seems as if the entire universe wants to see him and Purvi together and embarrass him.

On the way back, Purvi is all talks about Monisha. Vikram is thinking, first it was Monica Goswami (a friend of Purvi's who was against their liaison) in college days and now it is Monisha Goyal. Both the women shared the same initials - M and G. Is this a good sign? ONLY TIME WILL TELL.

Zindagi mein log aate hain, saza dene gaafil ....

Dukh deke badle mein, maza lene gaafil ...

Laga kar aag zindagi mein, denge hawa gaafil...

Khata bhi karenge, aur honge khafa gaafil ....

Vikram drops Purvi and goes home.

THE ROMANCE

Life moves on and Vikram and Purvi keep meeting regularly. There's a marriage in the family of Purvi's sister-in-law. Ramit (Purvi's husband) sends a car to pick Ananya, Chhotu, and Purvi. Purvi calls up Vikram and says she is going to Sheraton for a marriage and will not be able to talk to him in the evening. They will meet and talk the next day. Vikram says it's fine and goes home after office. He is having dinner when Purvi calls on WhatsApp. He is sitting with his family and doesn't want to pick her call; so, he lets it ring. Purvi calls again. This time he picks the phone since he doesn't want anyone to ask him to answer the call. Purvi says she wants to meet him and that he should come to Sheraton. Vikram knows it is not possible for him to go out once he has had dinner; but this is Purvi - she is not going to relent. So, he tells Anjali that he is going for coffee with a friend and leaves. On the way, he calls Purvi and asks if she is all right. She says she's not enjoying the company of her in-laws and that, she doesn't like Ramit being around. She also tells him that she has had four small drinks of vodka and is missing him (Vikram) now.

They are talking and Vikram reaches the Sheraton. He tells Purvi that he has reached and waiting for her in the valet area. Purvi comes and sits in the car. She is wearing a saree and is looking stunningly beautiful with a flower in her hair. They go for a drive. Vikram asks her if the kids know that she is with him. She says she has told Ananya that she was meeting Vikram and if anybody asks where your mom is, just tell them she must be here somewhere. Purvi holds Vikram very closely and puts an arm around his neck.

Vikram smiles; he knows she is drunk and can be bold right now. She kisses him on his cheek. They drive around for an hour and a half, talking, smiling, holding hands and kissing each other. Then, Purvi gets really bold and gives Vikram a smooch while he is driving. It's not easy to kiss while driving, but they do it anyways, and do it for long. It is around 11:45 pm and Purvi gets a call from Ananya, saying dadi is asking about you and that the party is almost over and they have to go. Purvi says she will be there in five minutes and asks Vikram to drop her back at the hotel. She is so very happy to meet Vikram and is still swinging because of the vodka shots she has had. Vikram stops the car in the valet area and before stepping out of the car, Purvi smooches him again. She looks at him, smiles, says 'good night jaan', and leaves. Vikram sees her going inside the hotel. She is looking so damn pretty and sexy tonight, and the kiss on the mouth, that was something Vikram loved right now. He drives back home, just thinking about her. She was being so nice to him that he keeps wondering what if they had been married 23 years back. What if…?

THREE CHEERS

Purvi is a compulsive talker. She has to be on phone all the time. After school or on holidays, irrespective of whatever she is doing, if she is not sleeping, she is plugged to her phone. If Vikram is busy with work, she talks to Monisha for hours. If Monisha is busy, she calls some other colleague or friend and talks. She talks while doing evening walks, she talks while doing school work, she talks while washing clothes, she talks while washing dishes, she talks while making tea, lunch, dinner, whatever she is doing. She is talking or messaging (she calls it multitasking and makes fun of Vikram, that he is bad at it). Her connect to any person is purely because that person has time to talk to her.

If Vikram doesn't talk to her for a few hours or doesn't meet her when she wants, she gets annoyed. Vikram has to appease her all the time and more than make up for the lost time. But with Monisha, it is a different story, maybe because they had been sharing things for a long time, and maybe because Monisha was a guiding force and kept all her secrets. One afternoon, Purvi calls Vikram to tell that she is going to Monisha's house for the day, and would not be able to talk to him. Vikram says it is fine with him, and that she should go and enjoy (how can he stop her from going). So Purvi goes to Monisha's house and they chill together. In the evening, Purvi calls Vikram and asks for his date of birth and the exact time of his birth. Vikram is surprised as to why Purvi is asking for these details (she knows very well when his birthday is), but he doesn't say anything and gives her the exact details. At around 8:45 in the evening, Purvi calls Vikram (he is driving back home from office) to ask if he can pick her from Monisha's place and drop her home. Vikram agrees and asks from where he has to pick her up. She gives him the address and asks him to call when he reaches there. Vikram drives towards Monisha's house and calls Purvi on reaching the given address. Purvi comes out of the house with Monisha and Vikram can see that they both are drunk. Monisha smiles and says hello. Vikram forces a smile and says hello too. Purvi comes around and sits in the car. Purvi looks at Vikram and says that next time, they will all sit together for drinks and dinner. Vikram just smiles at her. He waves his hand to Monisha (as if saying bye) and moves the car. He is driving slowly, for he wants to talk to Purvi. Purvi is inebriated, so he is hoping she might tell him what they had discussed (which normally she doesn't in Monisha's case). He wants to know about the secret of his date of birth.

Vikram asks Purvi how was her day, did she enjoy (which she must have considering she is drunk). Purvi looks at him, smiles, holds his hand and says it was wonderful. She tells him that she had gone in the afternoon and had lunch with Monisha. Then they slept for around two hours. In the evening, they sat in the bedroom and had some women talk (sex talk). Vikram wonders if they both are lesbians (the traits are there… they both enjoy discussing sex). Then they made vodka drinks for themselves and discussed about him at length while enjoying the drinks. She says, though she had already told Monisha their entire story from college time to this date, they talked about it again. Vikram can understand this; when one is drunk or emotional or excited, he or she tends to start the same story all over again (his friends do it all the time after getting drunk). So, similarly, the two women had discussed about him and his relationship.

What did Monisha say? asks Vikram. Purvi says that Monisha is happy that there was finally a man in her (Purvi's) life. She says that Monisha had been urging her to mingle with men. She also tells that Monisha has been saying that I have a very boring life; that I should have some amount of fun in my life; and that I was wasting my precious years managing school, kids, parents and home.

Vikram asks Purvi about his date of birth issue. Purvi is reluctant to tell, so Vikram asks her if everything in his horoscope was alright. Purvi says Monisha has an astrologer friend whom they consulted. He matched his and Purvi's horoscope and said they are compatible and would make a lovely couple. Vikram is surprised as to why Monisha is getting so involved with his association with Purvi. But silence is the key word.

Vikram is listening and nodding his head. This was getting interesting and he wanted to know all the details of their conversation. So, to encourage Purvi, he asks: So, you girls talked only about me all the time? No, no, no says Purvi. We discussed her (Monisha's) life too. She is having the time of her life. She is seeing two men simultaneously at this point of time. She is a very bold woman and has a thing for men. She is enjoying both the men. Her husband is not around much of the time, so she calls them and has sex with them and does all kinds of stuff with them. Vikram interrupts, what do you mean by all kinds of stuff? Purvi answers, all Kamasutra positions. She says when she (Monisha) will get bored, she will dump them and look for new opportunities. Vikram is wondering: Am I also such an opportunity for Purvi? Noooo. He reasons with himself, Purvi is not a sex addict like Monisha. She loves him. Purvi continues: Monisha has already had these kinds of flings so many times; and, I know about all of them.

Now this was a revelation. This was something Vikram wanted to know more about. This was alarming. He knows this woman (Monisha) is not right for Purvi. Having a friend of Monisha's type in your life, can be a disaster for you some day. The first and only time he had met Monisha, he didn't get positive vibes from her at all. A woman who has multiple flings can never be a good role model and a good advisor - of course, unless and until, you yourself are a playgirl. For Vikram, Purvi was a very plain and simple woman who didn't know the complexities of being a playgirl; and Monisha could never know what an emotional connect was, because for her, all relationships were sex-driven and not emotional. The worrying aspect was, that Purvi is sharing every detail about them with Monisha. How can he tell her not to; he should, but he can't. Sometimes, it's better to save your own relationship rather than pointing fingers at others. Especially when you know that the other person is going to feel offended by your advice.

Little did Vikram know, that in the long run, his keeping mum on certain issues was going to create bigger problems for him. One day, his carelessness was going to turn into a blunder. One day, his patience was going to ruin him. Not only would Vikram lose Purvi, he would also lose his self-esteem and self-respect. He would be tortured to such an extent, that he will be on the verge of losing his sanity.

THE OCCASIONAL OCCASIONS

Vikram and Purvi are happy together. They visit the guest house on a regular basis, minimum twice a week. Vikram avoids talking to Purvi about anything other than themselves. Occasionally they talk about Ananya or family members, but no mention of Monisha is made from Vikram's side. many a times, while returning from the guest house, Purvi calls Monisha and talks to her in their code language (it is usually yes or no from Purvi's side). Vikram sometimes tries to pay attention to make out what they are discussing; but he fails. He cannot understand what they are talking about and what Monisha is saying (or guiding). Asking Purvi about the conversation is not a viable option because he knows she is not going to tell. Many a times it happens that Vikram is driving and Purvi is talking and laughing over something with Monisha and they reach Purvi's house and their conversation is not yet over. What Purvi is sharing and what Monisha is advising is out of Vikram's understanding. Vikram is just happy that he gets to spend some quality time with Purvi in the guest house and that, at that time it is only Vikram and Purvi, talking, laughing, eating, drinking, doing whatever stuff, without any interference from anybody.

October-November are the months of Hindu festivals. Vikram and Purvi are together in the guest house on Dussehra eve. It's a holiday for both, so there's no binding of time. They go early in the evening and spend three hours together. Afterwards they go to a nearby dhaba and have dinner together. The food is spicy and delicious, and Purvi says they should visit this place more often.

After a few days, it is karwachauth. Purvi says to Vikram that she is fasting for his long life. She says she hadn't kept a fast in the last twelve years, but is keeping one today. She says her mom is surprised and happy at the same time. She says that mom is thinking that I am keeping the karwachauth fast for Ramit. Purvi's parents know what Ramit has done to their daughter, and that he has not only spoiled her life but also of their grand-children, Ananya and Chhotu. But, because they are getting old and because they care for Purvi and know well enough that they will not be there for her forever, they still hope that one day things will get right between Purvi and Ramit. The mother is specially very optimistic.

Vikram knows that the parents are not actually aware, that the fast is not for their son-in-law, but rather for someone, who could have been a son and a son-in-law and kept their daughter happy for life, had they not rejected him outrightly. Now their daughter was going to keep a karwachauth fast for the same man (Vikram), praying for his love and for his long life.

Though they are not a married couple, still, Purvi keeps a fast for Vikram's long and happy life. She says she always wanted to. She says now that the Gods have been kind enough to bless them with some happiness together, they should be thankful; and this was her way of thanking the Gods. Though Vikram has not asked her to keep a fast for him, he is happy that she thinks of him in such a way (treating him like a husband) and wants the best for him and has made him a part of her life. Since it is their first karwachauth together, Purvi asks Vikram to come in the evening to her house and help her complete the rituals (be there in person and offer her a glass of water to break the day long fast).

Vikram is in office when Anjali (Vikram's wife) calls. She asks him to come home early (before the moon rises), to help her break her fast by offering her water. Vikram is smiling to himself ... this is some sort of a sequence from a Govinda movie (Saajan Chale Sasural). Two women (both of them fasting for him, loving him and wishing for his well-being) want him to be there with them at the same point of time. How can that be possible? He has no twin brother and no duplicate of himself. But he has to manage, and manage he will...

Heer hain do, aur duvidha mein hai Ranjha gaafil....

dil hai ek, kis-se kare sanjha gaafil....

Kis-ko chhode, kis-se nibhaye gaafil....

Dono se hai mohabbat, kaise samjhaye gaafil....

In the evening, Vikram leaves from his office a bit early than normal. He had checked on Google, the time of the moon rise. It shows exactly at 8:10. So Vikram goes and parks his car at 114 at around 8:00 pm and calls Purvi. He tells her that he is waiting for her over there and that the moon will come up any time now. So, he asks her to come across the road in front of house number 114 with a glass of water so that she can see the moon and him together and break her fast. He sees Purvi walking out of her house and towards his car. She is wearing a white-colour suit and is looking beautiful as always. She is carrying a glass in one hand and a sieve in the other. She comes and stands by Vikram's car, looks at the rising moon through the sieve, spills some water on the ground while offering a prayer, and then immediately sits in the car. She looks at Vikram and smiles. Vikram offers her water; she takes a sip and hugs Vikram. Vikram's phone rings. It is Anjali. He picks up the phone and before Anjali can say anything, he says he is driving and will be home in 5 minutes. He keeps the phone and looks at Purvi. She is smiling and Vikram loves her smile. She hugs him again, thanks him for coming, and asks him to go as Anjali is waiting for him.

Vikram drives fast and reaches home in five minutes. There are a lot of women in the lane who are offering their prayers to the moon and their husbands are offering them water and breaking their fasts. Anjali is delighted to see Vikram. She is wearing a green-colour suit and looking pretty. She performs the same rituals Purvi had performed seven minutes back. Vikram offers her water and breaks her fast too. Then they go inside their house and Vikram makes a drink for himself (to relax) while Anjali is setting the dinner table. After he has enjoyed his two drinks, they all (Anjali, Vikram and the kids) sit and have dinner together. Vikram is all smiles while having dinner. He is relieved and somewhat happy that he managed both the fronts.

Diwali period is a bit hectic for all businesses because of its auspiciousness. Vikram is triple busy this year at this time. First, his business and family that keep him busy. Secondly, his friends and the card parties which keep him busy. Thirdly, it is Purvi and her love which is keeping him very, very busy. So much so, that in the name of going to card parties, Vikram is meeting Purvi instead and she is making it up with loving him more intensely. She doesn't want him to go to any parties or meet any friends because she knows his habit of losing big and winning big. She says it is better for him to stay away from such parties and enjoy with her instead. Even on Diwali night, this year, Vikram is not attending any card parties though he is invited to a couple of them. After the Diwali puja at home, he goes and picks Purvi and they both go to the guest house and enjoy drinks and dinner together ....

After Vikram drops her home and goes back, Purvi is sitting in the living room with her parents and kids discussing how her outing with friends was, when suddenly there is a loud bang in the driveway. The entire family rushes out to see what the sound was about. They see Mr Anand's (the first-floor family) son and daughter-in-law bursting crackers just outside the main gate, where their car is parked. The two families are not on talking terms and do not like each other. Purvi asks them to not burst crackers there as it is not safe and moreover, the main entrance is all getting messed up with the burnt-up crackers. They say it's an open space and nobody's personal area and they get into an argument. Purvi instantly calls the police and creates a ruckus outside her house. She makes Mr Anand's son apologise for being rude and misbehaving with her. The policemen warn him for his misconduct and leave. Purvi is immensely pleased with her triumph over the first-floor family.

THE FAMILY AFFAIR

Purvi has two elder sisters, Seema and Anita. Seema was married at a very young age, when she was only 19 and had just cleared her class 12 exams. She did her graduation after marriage. She now lives in Meerut with her lawyer husband and two sons. Her husband's name is Ajay and he is still angry with Mr Nand Kishore over the issue of the sale of his successfully running factories (he wanted one of them). He doesn't talk to his in-laws much and doesn't like visiting them. The other sister Anita is married to a Chartered Accountant. His name is Vivek and he works for an MNC. They live in Gurgaon with their son and daughter.

The two sisters visit their parents from time to time. Each time they visit, Purvi gets restless. She doesn't have good equation with the two elder sisters and has a feeling that they are always conniving to stake their claim in the parents' property, money, and jewellery. They do have small arguments from time to time and let down each other in front of the parents. Each time the sisters come to stay with the parents (Vikram is aware of the entire story as Purvi has told him everything about the sisters), he asks Purvi to stay away from arguments and advises her to stay mum and keep her cool. He is constantly in touch with Purvi and she updates him about every conversation she has with the sisters and the sisters have with the parents.

Seema stays in Meerut, so it is not possible for her to visit her parents frequently. So, whenever Anita plans to visit the parents, Anita informs Seema also and they come together and spend a few days with them. Purvi says Seema is a yes-woman of Anita; whatever Anita says, Seema cannot say no to it.

Anita's closeness with both the parents always bothers Purvi. Though Anita is very well off and her husband Vivek is getting a very handsome package (in crores per annum), still Purvi thinks that Anita has an eye on their mother's sarees and jewellery. Purvi always keeps an eye on her two sisters and whenever there is any discussion of jewellery and sarees between the two, Purvi always feels bad. After the sisters have left, Purvi always complains to mom and dad that the two sisters were rude and intolerable ...

In the January of 2014, Vikram is invited by Purvi to her house, to guide her two kids about their careers. Vikram is hesitant to go, but Purvi says that this was one good chance of meeting mom and dad. She tells her parents that one of her friend's husbands is coming over for a pep-talk with Ananya and Chhotu. In the evening, Vikram reaches her house and is received by Purvi at the gate. Vikram is a bit nervous but Purvi is very excited. This is the first time, Vikram is entering her house (a house which would have been his in-law's house, had he and Purvi got married) in her parents' presence. He remembers the Gods and thanks them, that finally he was meeting Purvi's parents. He had always wanted to see them, meet them, feel them, seek their blessings and in his own inner self, forgive them. Now, finally it was happening.

Vikram follows Purvi to the drawing room. It is large in size. There's an antique white dining table with glass table-top at one side and there's a seven-seater L shaped sofa on the other side of the room. The walls have a mirror (white-polished wooden frame in contrast with the dining table) and some paintings and photo frames. The overall look of the room is very royal, like they show in the movies. This is a huge house (500 sq yards) with very big rooms. Vikram is impressed.

The kids are sitting on a sofa in the room. Purvi asks Vikram to sit and goes to the kitchen to get him a glass of water. She goes to her parents' room and tells them that Vikram has arrived. Her mother accompanies Purvi to the drawing room. Vikram sees her mother and instantly falls in love with her. She is absolutely beautiful, with a wonderful smile, a creamy complexion and good features (Purvi is totally a copy of her mother). She is a magnificent woman with very regal looks. She still looks beautiful and has maintained herself despite the age (she is 70+).

Vikram goes forward and touches her feet to take her blessings. He asks her to put her hand on his head and bless him. The mother obliges. It is a wonderful feeling. What didn't happen then, was happening now. Vikram can't take his eyes off Purvi's mother. She is smiling at him, unaware that this man sitting across her, was the boy who was once denied entry in their house and in their lives.

Zamaana beet gaya, per bhool nahin paya gaafil ...

Kya dekh ke mujhko, kuchh yaad nahin aaya gaafil ...

hoon mein wohi, thukraya tha jisko ek din ...

waqt laya hai use, jise ishq nahin la paya gaafil ...

Vikram is talking to the kids and Purvi's mom is listening intently. The topic seems interesting to her, and she sits through the entire conversation. Afterwards, Purvi goes to the kitchen, makes tea and gets some biscuits along with it. She gives a cup each to her mom and to Vikram. Vikram is a bit shy in front of her mom and the feeling is like that of a boy who is sitting shyly in front of his to-be mother- in-law. Purvi goes and asks her father to join them for tea, but he doesn't want to. Maybe he is not comfortable in front of strangers. But Vikram is no stranger. He is the boy, Mr Nand Kishore had met 23 years ago and insulted and rejected. Now, he is losing an opportunity to meet that boy who had grown into a

43-year-old man, who still loved his daughter, and had forgiven him and his wife.

In the February of 2014, Purvi's mother starts feeling unwell. She has severe headaches from time to time. Purvi and her father take her to a doctor at Apollo Hospital. The doctor does a thorough check-up (MRI, CT scan, etc) and concludes that she has cancer. The doctor advises not to opt for any hardcore treatment (chemotherapy) as the mother was in the last stage and might not be able to fight the trauma and the tumour. They bring her back home.

The mother is at home, under medication. The sisters, Anita and Seema visit their home for a day, check on their mother, stay with the family the entire day and go back as they have to take care of their own families. Purvi is taking care of mother with the help of their servant and the nurse who they have hired for mother's assistance. Time passes but there's no improvement in mother's health; it is deteriorating day by day. So, Purvi, Anita and Seema discuss their mothers' condition on phone and decide that she should be given radiation and chemotherapy and she might get well and get cured. The father says what use is money of, if it cannot be spent for one's own wellbeing. They admit her to Max Hospital and the treatment begins.

One afternoon, Purvi is sitting in the hospital lobby trying to relax. She is tired of all the running around, so to take a break, she comes and sits in the lobby. She is scrolling through her phone, when a gentleman comes and sits beside her. After a while he says hello to her and asks her why she is at the hospital. Purvi replies that her mother is being treated for cancer. He says he is also there for his mother who is not well. Then he asks her what she does and she says she is a teacher in a Noida school. He says his nephew has to take admission in that particular school where she is teaching, and if she can guide and asks for her phone number. She gives him her mobile number and then leaves saying bye to that unknown person. Soon after, the man starts calling her over some pretext or other and starts stalking her. Purvi calls Vikram and narrates the entire story of this unknown man. Vikram is surprised as to how she can share her mobile number with a complete stranger who she had met in the hospital lobby. He asks her to simply block this man.

Purvi and Vikram are constantly in touch over phone. After her mother is admitted to the hospital, they have not met in person. Purvi has taken her due medical leaves from school and is looking after her mother. She is busy juggling between home and hospital. She has to look after her father, the kids, and the mother. The two elder sisters are of no help, except for asking about their mother's wellbeing over the phone. Vikram is Purvi's only moral support; she knows he will always be there for her whenever needed.

One day, while discussing her mother's health with Purvi, Vikram says he wants to pay a visit to the ailing mother and if he can come to the hospital. She says he can come any time he wants. That day, Vikram goes home after office, has dinner with his family and around 9:30 pm, he leaves for the hospital to visit Purvi's mother. He reaches the hospital and calls Purvi. She comes to the lobby with the attendants pass and takes him to the room on the second floor. It is a single-bed luxury room with all the amenities like TV, AC, sofa, extra bed for attendant, neat and clean English toilet....

Purvi's mother is sleeping. She looks like an angel with a smile on her face, even in sleep. Vikram doesn't want to wake her up and disturb her, so he quietly sits on the sofa. Purvi discusses her mother's health in hushed tones. Vikram sits for around half an hour and then gets up to leave. Purvi asks him to sit for a little while more. She has been sitting beside her mom and talking all this while. So, when Vikram says he is leaving, she makes him wait. Then she sits with him and starts cuddling him. He looks her in the eye, and smiles. He embraces her and kisses her on the lips. She says she wants him to stay with her and they can sleep on the attendant's bed together. Vikram says he doesn't want to disturb her mom and they kiss again. Before their kissing changes into something more intense, Vikram holds her face in his hands and asks for her permission to go home. Purvi is not happy; she wants him to stay, but she doesn't stop him. They get up; Purvi gives him a very tight hug, kisses him again and they leave the room together. Purvi sees him off in the lobby and goes back to her mother. Vikram goes home all smiles .... they had met almost after a week.

The unknown man who Purvi had given her mobile number to, is not discussed and not remembered, not remembered until the day when Vikram himself is accused of an act which he has not committed.

After a few days, Purvi's mother passes away. Vikram wants to attend the last rites and pay his last respects but is stopped by Purvi. She doesn't want anybody in the family to know about him. Vikram asks Purvi to at least inform her in-laws about the loss. She doesn't want to but then asks Ananya to inform her father about Nani's passing away. At the crematorium, her husband Ramit comes for a while and then vanishes without meeting anybody from the family. It doesn't surprise anybody as his visit does not matter to them. The sisters and their families are there, so are a few close relatives.

The family is deeply saddened by this sudden loss. Seema and Anita are staying back for a few days to be there with their grieving father. After a few days. Anita asks her father to come with her to her house or go to Seema's house for a few days. She thinks he needs some rest and a bit of a change as he is missing his wife a lot and is very sad. Purvi is aware of the conversation and asks her father not to go. She reminds him that none of the sisters were there to help when the mother was not well. She convinces her father that this was his only home and only she and her two kids were his family, and that he should not listen to those opportunity seeking sisters.

THE RICHES

After all the rituals, like the collecting of ashes from the crematorium and the last prayer meet for the departed soul are done, the two sisters Seema and Anita return to their homes with their families. They both had tried to persuade their father to come and stay with them for a few days, but he had very gently refused to go with any of them. Purvi updates Vikram about everything she has been going through. She knows, he backs her and believes her totally and will advise her correctly about any matter concerning her welfare.

On the other hand, Purvi starts brainwashing her father against the two elder sisters. Whenever she gets a chance, she reminds him that the two siblings are very well off and yet, still after father's money. She constantly reminds him that the two sisters were nowhere in sight when the mother was ill. She reminds him that how they had gone through those difficult times together (just Purvi and her father), and how they took care of mother together. She asks that now when mother is no more, who will take care of him and herself and the kids? They have to manage everything themselves and cannot depend on Seema and Anita.

One day while having dinner, Purvi discusses mother's gold and diamond jewellery and her very expensive sarees with father. She reminds him of the time last year, when Seema and Anita were here for a vacation, and had asked mother to show them her jewellery and sarees. After seeing the exquisite collection, they had both asked their mother to divide her collection properly between the three daughters while she was still alive. Purvi says that now, when mother is no more, and because she had taken good care of mother and will take good care of him too, she should be given the privilege to choose the jewellery and sarees and keep whatever she likes.

Father feels bad. He thinks Purvi is getting greedy and tries to reason with her. He tries to explain that her sisters are the only family she has. Once he is also gone, what other family will she have? So, he asks her to respect her sisters and love them, for they will be the ones who will look after her and take care of her and her two kids when he is no more.

But Purvi doesn't budge. She is not a person you can convince if she doesn't want to get convinced.

Every other day, Purvi starts discussing matters related to property or jewellery or sarees with her father. Mr Nand Kishore had bought a flat in the colony for Purvi, after she had separated from Ramit. He had thought that he would divide this big house among his three daughters and gift this three-bedroom flat to Purvi, so that at least she has a decent place to live in with her two kids.

NOW PURVI HAS OTHER PLANS.

She insists her father to sell this flat and give her the money. After a little persuasion, the father gives in. The flat is sold and money put in the bank in Purvi's name. The sisters are not immediately informed, but told in due course by the father who tells them that the flat had been sold because it had some plumbing and leakage issues. He said they are looking for some other property for Purvi and that she will settle there ultimately. However, the other property is never searched for. The topic of the new flat being bought or not was never raised either by the sisters (they got busy in their lives and almost forgot), or by Purvi and her father (why would they).

After his wife is gone, father is sad and a bit lonely. He misses his wife a lot. She was the one who looked after him and was a perfect companion. Purvi has other responsibilities like school, home, and her own kids to look after; so, she cannot be with father all the time. But thanks to Anil, the servant employed by the mother several years ago, Mr Nand Kishore is taken care of well when the kids and Purvi are not around. Anil is a caretaker-cum-butler.

LIFE GOES ON

Purvi had not stopped seeing Vikram, despite the tragedy in the family. She would sneak out of the house on some pretext or the other to meet Vikram and spend time with him in the guest house. She had been meeting him and going to the guest house with him regularly. After the mother is gone, it was getting tougher for her to move out of the house so frequently. Mother was good to her and never stopped her from socialising (mother felt sorry that the daughter was separated and didn't have a good life), but father was protective of her and didn't want her to go out so often. So, she decides to call Vikram to her house, instead of going to the guest house with him every third day. That way she would get to meet Vikram and also won't have to give excuses to her father for her late evening outings.

Moreover, they had been going to the guest house regularly for more than a year now. Purvi had been keeping a check on the expenses Vikram was bearing for this two-hour guest house stay, thrice a week. So, one day she says to Vikram that they have spent enough money on outings (the estimate came to more than Rs. Four lakh fifty thousand as calculated by her), and this was money spent only on the guest house. The other reason she cited was that Vikram was not paying attention to his business because of leaving office early. She wanted him to concentrate on his business too. She wanted him to know that she cared a lot for him. Vikram asks her how and where were they going to meet if not the guest house and she says, they can meet at her home itself. She says there is a bedroom in the front portion of the house, and it has two doors; one that connects it to the other portions of the house and the other one facing the front balcony. So, he can enter that room from the front without anybody in the family knowing that he is in the house. Vikram says it is okay with him as long as she was comfortable and happy.

Purvi had started sharing everything with Vikram. All the good advice she needed came from Vikram, for he was a wise man according to her. Purvi used to call him 'Google' for his immense knowledge. But all this jewellery, property, sarees' issue was handled and thought upon (maybe in consultation with Monisha) by Purvi herself. Vikram was only told about the action taken; never consulted on what was to be done as he was never interested in money-related talks or disputes. He always said that money spoiled relationships. So whatever Purvi told him, he approved of it thinking she was the most distressed of the three sisters and needed the house and money to survive.

A few days later, Seema and Anita visit their father and Purvi. The sisters planned the visit together as always (so that they all could meet). In the meanwhile, Purvi had brainwashed her father and told him to be straightforward with the sisters. The father was now totally dependent on Purvi for everything. He knew she had taken care of her mother but he never thought who else would have. Purvi was the one who was separated from her husband and living with them. So, it was easy for her to look after them. Seema and Anita had their husbands and kids to look after. How could he expect them to leave their families and stay over to look after mother or him for that matter. But the old man never reasoned and believed what he was made to believe. So, the sisters come but Mr Nand Kishore and Purvi are not happy to see them. Purvi is restless again. She and father had got mother's jewellery assessed in the absence of the sisters. It was divided into three parts, but the solitaires and more heavier and expensive things had already been taken by Purvi. The same had been done with the sarees. The ones Purvi wanted had already been taken by her, and the rest were hanging in the almirahs.

Anita sees Purvi wearing mother's solitaire earrings upon her return from the school. She is shocked to see that Purvi is wearing them without anyone's approval in the family. She asks Purvi that how she is wearing mother's earrings and Purvi very directly answers, that they were given to her by father and if she has any problems with that, then she should talk to him. That evening, while talking to father, Seema and Anita enquire about the jewellery and the sarees and ask father to divide it all fairly among the three sisters. They also ask him about Purvi wearing the solitaires. Father very bluntly says that he has given Purvi the solitaires to wear and that the jewellery has already been divided in three parts. Purvi has taken hers and they can have theirs. As for the sarees, he says they can go and choose from the almirahs for themselves.

The sisters get the message. IT IS LOUD AND CLEAR. You get what I give you. Seema and Anita don't have a choice and take whatever is left of the jewellery pieces and the sarees.

Khoon ke rishte bhi paani ho jaate hain gaafil ....

Daulat ke age bemaani ho jaate hain gaafil ....

Na rishte rahenge, na Daulat ek din ....

sab ban ke kahani reh jaate hain gaafil ....

BABY'S DAY OUT

Vikram is supposed to meet Purvi minimum twice a week at her house. Though Purvi wants him to come daily or on alternate days, it is not possible for Vikram to leave his home every day. The timings of their meetings are according to Purvi and they suit her completely. She always asks him to come after 10:30 pm in the night, when the kids have slept and daddy is in his room watching television or sleeping.

Leaving office and meeting Purvi in the guest house was easy for Vikram, for he would always reach home by dinner time. But going home and leaving after dinner was a very tricky situation. What would he tell his wife and his kids when leaving home? You just cannot keep telling them you are meeting friends after dinner. That was a lame excuse. Vikram knew they would not doubt him but he knew you cannot give the same excuses forever. The other factor he always has to keep in mind is that no-one sees him while entering Purvi's house from the front room and not the main entrance. It can dent Purvi's reputation. Anil, the servant, is one person Vikram has to watch out for. If he sees Vikram entering or exiting Purvi's room, he would definitely inform Mr. Nand Kishore, and that will be one serious issue. Secondly, the upper two floors are occupied by two different families and they keep coming and going at odd hours. If any of them sees Vikram entering the room or exiting it, it can again be problematic for both Purvi and him.

ONE DAY, ANIL THE CARETAKER-CUM-BUTLER IS TOLD BY PURVI THAT HIS SERVICES ARE NO MORE REQUIRED AND IS ASKED TO LEAVE.

Purvi starts getting bolder and more aggressive by each passing day. She has started experimenting things with Vikram (Hail Monisha!). Vikram asks her to refrain from performing certain tasks but she does not relent. He says love and lust are two different things, but Purvi has her own version: she says everything is fair in love and war. Once, during an argument over the same love and lust topic, she tears Vikram's shirt. Now, this is Vikram's and even her favourite shirt. Vikram is already angry over her desires and now seeing her tear apart his shirt, spoils his mood completely. He pushes Purvi aside and asks her not to talk to him ever again. He starts walking out in a huff. She tries to stop him and, in the process, his shirt buttons and a sleeve come apart. He stomps off in anger.

Vikram is driving back home when Purvi calls. He does not pick and she calls again. He doesn't want to pick the phone but then changes his mind and says hello. Purvi is sorry for her behaviour and wants him to come back to her. She starts pleading and crying. Vikram is a soft-hearted man and he loves Purvi. So, he takes the next U-turn and goes back to her. She hugs him for a long time and kisses him all over.

An almost same sequence will happen after five years, and Vikram will take a U-turn from the same spot. But that time, it will be a different story. That, in fact, will be the end of this wonderful story.

We know what has happened till now. But we don't know what is going to happen in the future.

Gar hota pata kal ka, toh khuda ho jaate gaafil ...

Khata na karte gar, kyun juda ho jaate gaafil ....

A few days later, Vikram is sitting with Purvi on the bed in the front room. They are enjoying their drinks and talking. Discussions are about normal day-to-day life, school, kids, business, family, relatives when suddenly, in between, Purvi says that she wants to have a baby. She says she has discussed it with Monisha and Monisha says it is possible. She says to Vikram that she wants to be the mother of his child; that she wants to get pregnant and bear his child. Vikram looks at her in amazement! What has getting pregnant got to do with love? He wonders, from where does she get these zany ideas, and can't help but think that Monisha is behind it all. They both have children who are 19-20 years old. Vikram looks at Purvi and smiles, absorbing what she had just said. Then, he very gently explains to Purvi that making a baby at this age and that too without getting married is a bad idea. What would her family think of her, what would the friends and colleagues say, how would the world react? He makes her understand and requests her to be reasonable and not act foolish. Purvi is upset for some time but then she gets back to normal, as even she knows that having a baby with Vikram is just not possible. For Purvi, the time had gone, but the desires are still there and for Vikram, the time has come, but the desires are all gone.

Things are moving fine. Vikram and Purvi are lovingly busy. Though there is no tension in Purvi's life, she is still constantly worried about the future. The kids are growing up, their education has to be taken care of, then they have to look for a career, then get married, then the house has to be rebuilt or renovated, the politics with the sisters is a never-ending affair. So, she is constantly worried about something or the other.

One Sunday afternoon, Purvi is cleaning the cupboards and almirahs to clear them of all the trash the kids and father have deposited in them. She is in the kids' room, clearing Ananya's drawer, when she sees a packet of condoms in it. She takes it out and checks if there are any condoms in there. It is an open packet and has two unused condoms in it. Purvi is aghast! She calls Ananya who has gone to a friend's house and asks her to come back home immediately. Ananya comes and tries to reason with her mother, but soon they both start fighting. Ananya has this bad habit of abusing and using all kinds of adjectives and she doesn't spare her mom this time either. Purvi slaps Ananya and goes to her room and starts crying. This girl is not mending her ways and always troubling Purvi. But what more can she do? She is a single mother who has raised both her kids independently, given them good education, good clothes, good food, and a decent life; and this girl is making life tough for her. Purvi calls Vikram and tells him the entire story. He asks her to calm down and rest for some time. To cheer her up, he says he will come to meet her in the night.

Purvi is upset and she shares the same Ananya story with Monisha. Monisha asks her to relax and come down to her house to spend the evening with her. She says that way they can meet and also have a drink together. Purvi likes the idea and goes to Monisha's house. There they discuss all that Purvi has been going through for the last few days and what Monisha has been up to. They have drinks together and spend the entire evening drinking and talking.

Purvi calls Vikram at around 9 pm and asks him to pick her up from Monisha's place. Vikram doesn't like her meeting Monisha or her going to Monisha's place, but he doesn't say anything. He goes at the appointed time to pick her up. On the way, he doesn't talk much. This time, he doesn't ask her what they did, or what they talked about. He is no more interested. He knows that Monisha has more influence in Purvi's life than him.

Keh denge toh, kho denge usko ....

Na kahen, toh kho denge khud ko ....

Bhali hai Khamoshi, zalalat se gaafil ...

Na denge dosh, hum kabhi bhi tumko ....

When you love someone, you don't want to hurt their feelings; and Vikram was a person who loved the world. He would never hurt anyone in any way. He respected everybody in their own right and maintained dignity in his relations.

ADULTERY

In the summer of 2016, Ananya completes her graduation and gets a job with an MNC. On weekends, Ananya usually goes partying with her friends. Purvi, along with Vikram, drops her and picks her from the venue. In between dropping and picking up Ananya, Purvi and Vikram themselves go to different places for dinner. That way, Purvi is assured that the girl is at the right place with the right friends (that she is not lying) and she herself can spend some time with Vikram (meeting in the first room has restricted their outings).

Ananya is now busy with her office work and it seems that her problems with Purvi are more or less over. There is no news of her misbehaving with her mom, or getting drunk, or going on dates with boyfriends without informing her mom.

IT IS NOT ANANYA WHO IS GOING ON A WRONG TRACK THIS TIME. THIS TIME IT IS HER MOTHER, WHO IS GOING OUT OF A RELATIONSHIP AND MEETING SOMEBODY. SOMEBODY OTHER THAN VIKRAM ...

One Saturday (normally school is shut on Saturdays), she calls Vikram and says she will be busy for some time and would not be able to talk. In that time, when she is supposed to be busy, she goes to Connaught Place (CP) to meet an old friend of hers. A man named MR. DHAM. They have been friends for last fifteen years and have kept in touch. She hasn't told Vikram much about this man. She had once very casually mentioned his name to Vikram, telling him that Dham was an old friend and even her husband

Ramit knew him well. She had told Vikram that she felt that Dham liked her. Vikram had smilingly avoided the topic. He was not interested in her infatuations anymore. This was the fifth man (apart from the THREE WOMEN who, she said, loved her body - all three of them were colleagues from school. The women just loved Purvi's curves and wanted to do one-to-one with her) who was interested in her and was being mentioned in the last four years. MORE WERE YET TO COME.

The first was a music teacher from the same school, where she was teaching. The masterji had the habit of checking her out every time he saw her. He used to play saxophone with his eyes whenever he saw Purvi and used to look for excuses to feel her.

The second was a mobile shop employee. She had gone to get her phone repaired and got overfriendly with the sales person (she also gave him her phone number). The guy used to call her and express his respect (love) for her. He used to tell her that if she needed any help ever, he would be always there.

The third was the hospital man, who she had met in the hospital lobby. Again, the phone numbers were exchanged and the man was blocked after he tried to get more than friendly.

The fourth was a parent of a kid from her class, whom she got acquainted to during the parent teacher meeting. Either the parent was desperate or Purvi; for they would chat on WhatsApp (everyday) on the pretext of the child's studies and homework.

Then there was a school colleague`s husband who she had met at another colleague`s wedding. The man checked her out throughout the evening. She saw him staring at her and trying to get friendly even in his wife`s presence.

THIS WAS THE SIXTH MAN, MR. DHAM.

Vikram didn't like prodding Purvi. His philosophy was simple, if she wants to share, she will. If she doesn't want to share, she won't. So, it was like live and let live. Do not interfere. So, when Purvi mentioned Dham's name, Vikram was not interested.

Purvi had on numerous occasions told Vikram that he didn't know how to draw her latent feelings out. But he simply didn't care. He didn't care about other people's stories. He was only interested in Purvi and his story. About their story, he used to say: One day, I am going to author a book on our love. The only thing stopping him to start writing was the END; because the story was still in motion. How could he put an end to it? It was such a wonderful story, that any loving person who is in love, would not like it to end. So, he always said to himself that he would wait. The story has to have a happy ending, like in movies. THE POOR FELLOW KNOWS THAT NOT ALL STORIES HAVE A HAPPY ENDING, SOMETIMES IT'S TRAGIC TOO. BUT HE IS SURE HIS WON'T BE ANY OF THOSE.

So Purvi goes to CP and meets Mr Dham in a pub. They greet each other, shake hands, sort of semi-hug each other and take a table. Mr Dham orders beer and some snacks for both of them. They get talking and discuss how they both are doing in life. In between they are enjoying their beer and snacks. The conversation is only about the two of them.

Purvi knows that Mr Dham likes her. He had said so himself, so many times on phone and WhatsApp. But what she probably doesn't know is, any woman who is separated from her husband, or is divorced, or is a widow, and is young enough (44 is not old and Purvi looked very pretty and very sexy), looks good enough (Purvi had maintained herself) .... is always loved and liked by men. She is not liked because of her qualities; she is liked because she is an opportunity. An opportunity for a middle age companionship, a middle age fling, middle age sex. An opportunity because she is single again and is lonely with nobody to love her, nobody to share, nobody to take care and nobody to provide that ring of security which a husband provides. The world thinks she is ready to mingle. Any man knows that a separated single woman is an easy target. Mr Dham also knew this very well. He had been prying on her for a long time. He knew she was separated. He knew she was younger to him. He knew she was approachable; and, he knew she liked him. They had been friends for so long and she had always responded in a very positive way. Even yesterday, when he called her and asked her out for lunch and drinks, she had said yes instantly. He knew, Purvi won't say no ....

Only Vikram didn't know what was going on between the two of them, what all they talked about and what messages they shared. Vikram was such a careless man, that he never thought about Purvi's liaisons with other men. She had many admirers which she used to tell him teasingly about, but Vikram thought Purvi was merely trying to make him jealous. He loved her and he thought she loved him even more. So, whenever Purvi mentioned about some other man, Vikram took it very casually and overlooked the real scenario. He was mentally not prepared to accept, that she could fall for some other man (which she did eventually).

Purvi often used to tell Vikram that there were things that he didn't understand about their relationship, and Vikram would always say that if she won't tell him, how would he know what it was? BUT SHE NEVER OPENED HER HEART TO HIM. She said she and Monisha were close because Monisha understood everything, even without her (Purvi) telling her anything. Vikram always got confused; he could not understand a woman's psyche. What were the things which Monisha could understand and he could not? He always thought about it but could not make out what it was.

He could not get it, that she was a single woman who had been separated for about fifteen years now.

He could not get it, that she needed companionship.

He could not get it, that love was not enough.

He could not get it, that a woman who was being pursued by so many men, is bound to have secret desires.

He could not get it, that a woman could go out of a relationship which was purely about love and had nothing to do with physical needs.

HE WAS A CARELESS MAN. A GAAFIL.

These were the times of WhatsApp, Facebook, Instagram and all kind of exposure to social media. Things which were not new to the world were all new to Vikram. He had downloaded WhatsApp in 2013 and still did not have a Facebook account, leave alone other social media apps.

This was a man who was born in the seventies and grew up watching Rajesh Khanna movies.

This was a man who loved Lata Mangeshkar songs.

This was a man who still believed in first love.

This was a man who never once fell for a woman in his entire life, other than Purvi.

This was a man who was liked and loved by a lot of women, but who never took notice of their glances and advances.

He was busy in his own world - the old world. In between Purvi leaving him and meeting him again, he was a complete family man. A man dedicated to his wife and two kids. Never did he think that life will change tracks and take a course that was so unpredictable.

SO PURVI AND MR DHAM ARE ENJOYING THEIR DRINKS AND HAVING A LOVELY CONVERSATION. Mr Dham has been an admirer of Purvi from the time they had met. He always liked her curvaceous figure and dreamt of making out with her one day. He knew somehow that even Purvi liked him, and here was a solid proof. Why would a woman come to a pub and enjoy drinks with a man she doesn't like or is not interested in? He knew he just had to make the next move and the woman was all his. But what he didn't know was, a woman is to be loved. She is to be pursued. She is to be told in a very gentle manner, what you desire from her.

That's where Mr Dham made a mistake.

Instead of moving slowly and making a connect with Purvi and taking some time before asking for the penultimate, Mr Dham told Purvi that he loved her and wanted to have sex with her.

Any woman with some amount of self-respect, will not take kindly to these words. Neither did Purvi.

She also wanted to have fun. She also wanted to do all things with Mr Dham. She knew that this was a man who had been friends with her for so long, that the relationship could be taken to another level. But she didn't like the way he proposed to have sex with her. He should have been a gentleman. He should have taken some time to get comfortable with her. She was ready for all the pleasures. She was ready for sex. But she was not ready for the treatment meted out to her just now. This man had blurted the SEX word as if she was a woman who is easily available.

Dhokha na de khud ko, hai duniya matlab ki ....

Parwah na hogi teri, teri mohabbat ki ....

Na de tasalli khud ko, dum tera bharti hai ....

Mohabbat hai tere badan se, usi pe marti hai...

Purvi looked around in embarrassment and in disgust. It seemed as if all the people sitting around were staring at her, as if she was available to all. Purvi got up there and then. She didn't even bother to say bye to Mr. Dham and just ran out of the pub. She was a little drunk, but still in her senses. She could not believe what she had just heard. This man thought of her as a mere sex object. This meeting was thought to be a beginning of a new chapter in life, a new beginning of wild desires to be fulfilled (something that Vikram was not offering). But it turned out to be a dud, a complete rout of expectations. Purvi goes home full of frustration and anger.

That day, she didn't talk to Vikram. Vikram called her twice and both times she said she was busy with school work and would talk later. Once, she was in the pub with Mr. Dham and couldn't talk, and the other time, she just didn't want to talk out of frustration and anger. Vikram loves her, but is not adventurous and bold. On the other hand, this Dham guy was too bold and too straightforward for her comfort level. She is in no mood of talking to both the guys. LOVE GOES FOR A TOSS AND DESIRES CONSUME ALL HER ATTENTION.

VIKRAM knows that whenever Purvi is busy with schoolwork, she will not talk. So, this time when she says that she was busy with some project, Vikram doesn't say anything. He just hangs up and thinks tomorrow is always a better day, a better prospect. He knows that when she will get tired or bored with the burden of too much work, she herself will call. But she doesn't.

Vikram calls Purvi the next day and she sounds tired; maybe she has worked till late in the night. So, to lighten up her mood, Vikram asks her if she would like to go for a drive or for dinner with him. He knows she needs a break. Even Purvi wants to freshen up her mood and get over with what had happened yesterday at the pub. She tells Vikram that they can go for a drive and dinner.

In the evening, at around 9:30 pm, Vikram picks Purvi up from her house, at the regular spot. On the way, he stops at a wine shop and buys four pints of beer. Then they drive towards a colony market and park the car in front of a dhaba. This dhaba guy serves food in the car and is famous for his non-veg delicacies. Vikram calls the waiter and orders a plate of tawa chicken with rumali rotis.

Purvi is normally very talkative and very cheerful, but today she is very quiet. Vikram gives her a pint; they say cheers and start drinking. The first two pints are gone in few minutes. They both gulp the beer as if they both were very thirsty and it was water instead of beer. There was some tension on Purvi's face when Vikram had picked her from her house, but after the first pint, she looks a bit relaxed. Vikram opens the remaining two pints and gives one to Purvi. They are not talking; Vikram is constantly looking at her face. It is so innocent that Vikram wants to hold her in his arms and kiss her. But Purvi is avoiding eye contact; she is looking outside blankly. Normally Purvi doesn't do this. She loves Vikram looking at her. She blushes and smiles every time he looks into her eyes. But this time, she is just sitting in the car, inattentive to Vikram's lovey-dovey eyes. Vikram is not liking this silence, so he asks her if everything is fine with her. Now Purvi looks at him, forces a smile and says it is all ok.

By the time they finish their second pint, the waiter gets the food. They eat silently. It is only 10:20 pm and they are through with drinks and dinner. Vikram doesn't want to go home so early, and he is in no hurry of dropping Purvi early either. He wants to sit with her and talk. He has this feeling that Purvi wants to say something, so he is waiting for her to begin. He is all ears to whatever she wants to share. So, he starts the conversation.

Vikram: You're very quiet today. Is everything all right?

Purvi: Yeah, all good. Just a bit tired and some heaviness. Otherwise, all good.

Vikram: Do you want to sit for a while and talk, or shall we move?

Purvi: We can sit. I am in no hurry and am also not feeling like going home.

Vikram: We haven't talked the last two days. Please do share what you were busy with?

Purvi loves Vikram, but then she loves herself too. In fact, she loves herself more than she loves Vikram. She loves the attention she has been getting lately from other men and women. She has been deprived of so many pleasures of life for last so many years. She had been living a very lonely and colourless life and nobody cared. Now when life is giving her a chance, she wants to make the most of it. Of course, Vikram is there and he loves her, and he has been around for almost three years now, but his love and affection are not enough. It is not fulfilling. Purvi wants to explore. She wants to fulfil her sexual desires; she wants to experience things not virtually, but in reality.

She does not shy away from telling Vikram what had happened yesterday. She is so in control of herself, her body and her mind right now, that all these things (the Dham episode) appear very normal to her. She shares the story with Vikram so casually, as if there is no significance to it.

She starts narrating .... Yesterday morning, I got a call from Dham. You remember I told you about him, that we have been good friends and even Ramit knew about him. So yesterday he called and said that he wanted to meet; he had something important to discuss. So, we decided to meet at CP in the afternoon. I went to a pub where he was waiting and had lunch and drinks together. After a few drinks he got high and while we were conversing generally, he proposed me out of the blue and said he loved me and wanted to have sex with me. I was outrightly offended and I left the place and returned home. I immediately blocked him on my phone and swore that I will never talk to him... Asshole ....! I was having a severe headache (hangover) in the evening so slept early, that's why I didn't talk to you.

THE STORY DID GET A LITTLE BIT TWEAKED IN BETWEEN.

The waiter comes and the bill is settled. Vikram lights up a cigarette and takes a drag. He has nothing to say. There is no thought process; he is blank. He is obviously HURT; but he doesn't want to show it or say anything about it. Vikram has always made sure that, no matter what, he is not going to argue or fight with Purvi. He will just surrender. Let her win. Let her have the feeling of control. Let her think that she will never be wrong and he will never be right. Let her feel that nothing will go wrong in her life again.

So, he asks her if they should head home now and she says yes. Vikram is driving and Purvi holds his hand as always and rests her head on his shoulder. Now this is always a wonderful gesture by Purvi. Usually, he loves it. But not today. Today he is still blank and thoughtless. He stops the car at 114. Purvi gives him a tight hug and a kiss and says bye. He says bye with a forced smile. She goes inside her house. He watches her going as if she was taking his soul with her.

Dard baantne aaye the, zeher pee ke chale gaafil....

Humein maut, aur aap zindagi jee ke chale gaafil ....

Vikram reaches home and parks his car just outside his house. He doesn't feel like going inside, so lights up a cigarette and just keeps sitting in the car. Vikram has always abided by one principle: Whatever tensions the outside world gives you, they are not to be carried home. He is tense right now. He takes a drag and his mind goes on a self-drive mode ... There are so many questions that his mind is trying to find answers to. Why did Purvi lie to him? Why did she not tell him where she was going and with whom and for what purpose? If it was supposed to be a friendly lunch or a business meeting, how come it turned out to be a blind date? What prompted Dham to propose her and ask for sex? That too, in a restaurant? Things were not connecting. Purvi was hiding something. Why did she go and meet him in the first place? Why did she have drinks with him? What physical signals did she give him while having drinks that he got so direct with her? One has to have balls to tell a woman in the first meeting itself - that too, in a crowded pub - that you want to have sex with her. Whoosh! This guy was so tacky (or was he not).

PURVI HAD A COMPLETE SAY IN VIKRAM'S LIFE; TOTAL CONTROL. She was the one who decided everything for him. She had asked him to stop talking to Rupam and other friends, which he had done. She didn't want her family (her sisters and Vikram had some common friends) to know about them, which he completely understood and took care of. She didn't want him to go for parties and dinners (and spend time with her instead), which he had stopped going for. So much so, that he neglected his wife, his children, his family, his business and even his health to keep her happy. He had done so much for this woman he loved more than anything in his life, and she had no compunction behaving so casually about him. He could not understand that if she was already in a romantic relationship with him, why did she go to meet Dham? Was there more to this story of hers and Dham? VIKRAM HAD TEARS IN HIS EYES. It had been an hour that he had been sitting in the car outside his house. Now it is already 1:00 am and he is too lonely, too tired, and too sleepy to sit in the car anymore. He goes home and tries to sleep.

Daga na kar gaafil, ki mohabbat hai tujhse ....

Rooth jaaoon, chhod jaaoon, na hoga mujhse ....

Tu le imtihaan, ki kamzor nahin honsle apne ....

Toot jaaoon, bikhar jaaoon, lad jaoon khud se ....

Tu daga na kar gaafil, mohabbat hai tujhse ....

THE ONE QUESTION THAT WAS BOTHERING HIM WAS ... why didn't she tell him beforehand .... before going to meet Dham.

VIKRAM LEAVES IT AT THAT AND SLEEPS ON THE MATTER, FOREVER.

Now this was where Vikram went wrong. He just could not believe that anybody he loved so much could betray his trust. He just could not believe that Purvi could betray him. He loved her too much, trusted her too much, respected her too much. He didn't know that this was just the beginning of what was to happen in near future. The beginning of a woman going out with someone other than him. The beginning of treating him like a yes-man. The beginning of love for other men and women turning into lust. THIS WAS THE BEGINNING OF VIKRAM TURNING BLIND IN THIS RELATIONSHIP. Vikram believed in the theory of eternal love; and love for him also meant to let go. He never told Purvi that she was wrong, because there was a promise to keep. The promise of loving her unconditionally and being with her always, even if it meant bowing to the wrongs committed by her. This was where he was encouraging her unknowingly, for, the woman started taking him for granted. She knew he was too emotional and too attached to her that he won't go anywhere in spite of her misdeeds.

This was where Vikram should have taken a stand and made things clear to Purvi. He should have told her that if she had no control over her floundering ways, their relation was more than over. He should have been strong, and maintained a distance. He should have at least tried to detach himself emotionally.

BUT HE DIDN'T. HE WAS WEAK. HE WAS EMOTIONAL. HE LOVED HER.

This was the first thing that went wrong on Purvi's part and still accepted by Vikram as normal. That is what paved the way for what happens with him four years later. A COMPLETE MURDER

OF HIS CHARACTER, HIS SELF RESPECT, HIS LOVE AND DIGNITY. An outcome, which no one could have thought of, ever. but Vikram was a careless man. A GAAFIL.

THE CONFUSION

THIS WAS NOT THE FIRST TIME IN THE WORLD THAT A MAN WAS GOING OUT OF HIS MARRIAGE AND HAVING AN AFFAIR WITH A WOMAN. Vikram was a wise man. He knew what he was doing. He knew there would be consequences. But he could not help it, for he had always loved PURVI. And love is not a good thing to happen to good people. If it is a success, it results in marriage. And if it is not successful, it results in a heartbreak. Heartbreak it was for Vikram back then, after which he had spent the last twenty-three years in getting together those pieces of his broken heart. And now when Purvi was back in his life, his heart had a life.

THIS WAS ALSO NOT THE FIRST TIME THAT A MARRIED WOMAN WAS HAVING AN AFFAIR WITH A MAN. But the thing was, Purvi was trying to go around with more than one man at a given time, and this was a big problem in itself. ANY MAN OR A WOMAN WHO IS IN AN EXTRA-MARITAL LOVE AFFAIR, CANNOT TOLERATE THEIR BELOVED TO HAVE ANOTHER RELATIONSHIP WHILE KEEPING YOU AS A STANDBY.

THIS IS NOT THE CODE OF LOVE. Even love has to have some discipline, a decorum. Here, there was no decency, no code, and no discipline. Every relationship has a protocol, which has to be respected and followed religiously. BUT HERE, ALL THE RULES WERE FOR VIKRAM ONLY. Purvi was free from any kind of commitment. She made sure she knew everything about Vikram. His daily routine, his movement, who he was talking to, how was the business, what he was eating, what time he woke up and what time he slept. BUT, WHEN IT CAME TO BEING TRANSPARENT ABOUT HERSELF, SHE NEVER LET ANYTHING OUT OF THE BAG.

Nevertheless, a few days later, everything is normal again. Vikram is meeting Purvi at her house as usual and as normally as he can. Dham is never discussed again. Vikram is least interested in Purvi's antics. It is that time of the year when Vikram used to go for Diwali card parties (which normally starts a month and a half in advance) and play big. Last two years he had stopped going because of Purvi. This year he wants to go for a change of mood and routine, and for making up with the rest of the friends. He goes to a party and as luck would have it, meets a college friend Manoj. They sit together for a while, enjoying their drinks and smoking cigarettes, catching up on good old days. They are sharing with each other, the stories of life after college and telling each other what they had achieved in life so far, when out of the blue Manoj asks Vikram about Purvi: Did you marry Purvi? he asks Vikram. Vikram looks at him, smiles and says: Her father was a rich man, bro. How could he get his daughter married to a middle-class boy like me? But it's okay, this is what life is. The friend smiles and says: "Rich man …Sanjeev (a college friend) was telling me the other day that you have made good money and are doing very well for yourself. But good for you, you didn't marry Purvi". Vikram looks at Manoj in disbelief! Who is this man to say what is good for me and what's not? Manoj continues "the girls in college used to say that she was too moody and too obsessed about herself. A kind of psycho". Vikram is speechless. He does not want to refute his claim and drag this conversation about Purvi any further. He finishes his drink, says bye to Manoj, and leaves.

Monisha is a big part of Purvi's life. Everything is shared and discussed by the two on a daily basis. Whatever they discuss and talk, is never shared with Vikram except that one time when Purvi was drunk and she told Vikram about Monisha's sexual soirees because she herself wanted to have those sexual urges of hers fulfilled by Vikram. BUT IT WAS NOT TO BE. VIKRAM always insisted that there had to be some difference between love and lust. AND PURVI NEVER AGREED. She used to say it was all part of love and there was nothing called lust.

One fine day, when Vikram was to meet Purvi at night, Purvi told Vikram that she had invited Monisha to her place and that the three could have drinks and dinner together. Monisha is a bad influence in Purvi's life, but Vikram cannot say this to Purvi. He doesn't want any confrontation in his relation with Purvi. He doesn't want his relation to go bad. But, the consequences of Vikram avoiding these major issues will be huge one day … HUGE!

Ikaththa kiye apni, barbadi ka samaan hum ….

Kuchh keh na sake, dete the tum pe jaan hum ….

Jo hota gumaan, ki jaan hi le logi gaafil ….

Toh aane na dete kabhi, zindagi mein tufaan hum ….

That night, when Vikram reaches Purvi's house and calls her, he is told by Purvi that they won't be sitting in the front room and instead in the master bedroom in the back. She tells him that there's a way to the master bedroom from the servant quarters and he has to come from there. Vikram walks through the driveway to the servant quarters, crosses it and there's the back door entry to the master bedroom. The room is dark with no lights on and only the moonlight pouring in through the windows. Purvi doesn't want to be disturbed by daddy or the kids, so no lights and moreover, she doesn't want them to know that Vikram has joined them. They are sitting on the bed and enjoying their drinks (both of them are two pegs down each) when Vikram enters. He says hello to both and makes a small drink for himself and sits on the other side of the bed. He lights up a cigarette and Monisha says that she wants to share the cigarette with him. Vikram takes a drag and gives it to

Monisha. She holds it in between her small finger and ring finger in true Akshay Kumar (Bollywood star) style and takes a drag. The women are discussing the same old shit of how they met and how they got to be so close over the years. Vikram knows it all (Purvi has told him umpteen times) but is still listening. Vikram makes his second drink and lights up a cigarette again. Monisha again asks to share. By this time, the two women are four drinks down each and are drunk.

Vikram asks Purvi if they had ordered any food. She says she will go to the kitchen and get it. She asks him to lock the door from inside and goes out. Vikram locks the door and comes and sits on the bed. Monisha says she is feeling sleepy. She lies on the bed and closes her eyes. The posture she is lying in is very tempting, very inviting, as if she wants Vikram to come on top of her, and do it to her. She is a woman who has been very adventurous and very bold. She is the one who changes men more frequently than men change their wardrobes. She is a mentor to Purvi and her guiding force. Maybe she is trying to tempt Vikram or is testing his patience. But this man is madly in love with Purvi. He has not even dreamt of any woman other than Purvi. The room is dark and there are only the two of them in the room. Monisha is fully drunk and Vikram half drunk. Vikram looks the other way and thinks how much time is Purvi going to take to bring the food.

Five minutes pass by. Monisha is lying on the bed and Vikram is sitting by her side all alone in this dark room with no lights on, waiting for Purvi. Time is ticking by... ten minutes .... fifteen minutes .... twenty minutes. Purvi is still not back. Vikram is sitting in the dark, alone, with Monisha sleeping at his side. Those twenty minutes are the longest he has experienced in forty-seven years of his life. Finally, Purvi knocks on the door. Vikram heaves a sigh of relief and opens the door. She keeps a few things on the bed and goes back towards the kitchen asking him to lock it again. Vikram tries to wake up Monisha by telling her that dinner is ready. But she doesn't move. She is dead drunk and dead asleep. Two more minutes and Purvi is back in the room. She asks him if all was fine; he says it is. The food is ready, so Vikram goes to the washroom to wash his hands. Purvi swingingly follows him and while he is washing his hands, she embraces him from behind. They are in the washroom for about five minutes and when they get back to the room, MONISHA IS GONE. SHE HAS VANISHED.

Just five minutes back, this woman was drop dead drunk and asleep, and now she is nowhere to be seen. Purvi is neither surprised nor shocked to not find her in the room. The kind of camaraderie the two women shared, Purvi should have gone mad on not seeing her, but she is not showing any concerns. Monisha was supposed to stay for the night at Purvi's place and now she's gone. It is 12:45 in the night and Vikram is wondering, where could Monisha go at this time. Purvi asks him to relax and eat dinner. They sit and eat dinner together. Vikram stays for a while and then leaves for home.

On the way, he is thinking that there is something fishy about Monisha. He has just met her twice and already he doesn't like her. The woman acts to be too outwardly smart. She wants to have one upmanship on whatever the discussion is and the same qualities she was trying to imbibe in Purvi. Of late, Purvi had started acting like her too.

The next day, Purvi is talking to someone when Vikram calls. she calls back a little while later and says she was talking to MONISHA. Vikram asks Purvi about what had happened last night, where had MONISHA gone. PURVI says that MONISHA told her that her husband was going home from office and thought of picking her on the way. So, she went back home with him. (This is a lie.)

Who was lying to whom? Was MONISHA lying to PURVI, or was PURVI lying to Vikram, or were they both lying and cooking up a story? MONISHA WAS TO STAY FOR THE NIGHT. MONISHA was sleeping. Vikram had gone to the washroom, Purvi followed him there, they spent a few minutes inside, the door was open. They didn't hear any phone ringing, they didn't hear MONISHA talk to anyone on phone and yet, when they came out, she was gone. If she was so drunk and so fast asleep that she couldn't even move and reply to Vikram when he asked her for dinner, how come she got up all by herself, received the muted call and leave without informing PURVI? The dots did not connect. (Some matters you just have to leave; you don't have to understand everything happening around you. If it is SHIT happening, let it happen). Vikram could not get it. How could he? The man was so occupied with the thought that where did MONISHA vanish, that not once did it occur to him, that why did Purvi leave him with Monisha in the room all alone for more than twenty minutes, when she could not even tolerate him sitting with his own wife (she does not like it and she doesn't want him to spend time with Anjali).

ALL GIRLS SOIREE

It is the summer of 2017, and things are just moving fine. ANANYA has gone to a friend's house and Purvi is busy with school work and her mobile phone. She is planning to make Chicken Masala for dinner, so she decides to go to the market and buy chicken. She goes to the meat shop, buys chicken and is coming out of the market when she sees ANANYA standing with a male friend in the market. They are both touching each other while talking and it does not go down well with PURVI. She calls ANANYA on her phone and asks her where she is. Ananya says she is with Diksha (a colony friend) and will come back home after lunch. Purvi does not like that Ananya is lying to her, and this is not the first time. The more Purvi wants to have faith and trust in Ananya, the more this girl lies to her. So Purvi rushes to the spot where Ananya is hanging out with this boy-friend of hers and gives her a tight slap on her face in full public view. The boy just vanishes. On the way back home, while taking the car out of the parking lot, Purvi has an argument with the parking attendant and she calls the police. The poor guy is given a good verbal (full of abuses) lesson by her and the policemen. After that, Purvi brings Ananya home and the two get into a verbal fight again.

Purvi goes to her room and wonders where her life is going. Mom was no more, daddy was getting older and weaker, sisters were of no help, Ananya was a constantly trouble-giving child, Chhotu was growing up and had stopped listening to whatever she said, the Dham episode was over, Vikram was boring, and Monisha was the only one who gave her some hope. She was the one who understood her perfectly and guided her properly. So, she calls Monisha and they talk for nearly two hours. Monisha asks her to spice up her life. She asks Purvi to stop caring about the world and live life as she wants to. She updates Purvi about her own life and the men she is enjoying with. PURVI DECIDES TO ADD SOME COLOUR TO HER DULL AND BORING LIFE.

Purvi calls Vikram and asks him to take her for a holiday. Some place where they can go, relax and enjoy for a couple of days. Vikram is in a fix. It is not easy for him to leave his business and family and go on a leisure trip. He takes time out just once a year to take his family for holiday. Purvi knows this very well and is still asking him to take her somewhere. Vikram wants to, but he cannot. Moreover, he does not want to lie to anybody in the family about where he was going and with whom. So, he explains his reluctance for going on a holiday with her and she is not happy about it.

A few days later, Purvi informs Vikram that she is going to Amritsar tomorrow, for two days with a few friends of hers. Vikram says he is happy for her and that she should go and enjoy. This is a much-needed break for her. He asks her who are the friends she was going with and she says they are school colleagues and names them all. They are four women and have already made the travel arrangements and booked the hotel. Purvi asks him to come and meet her before she goes, for she will not be able to even talk to him when she is with her friends. Vikram goes and has dinner with her and spends some time with her just to make her happy.

The next morning, PURVI and her friends take the train to Amritsar and reach there by afternoon. Purvi is updating about the journey to Vikram on WhatsApp. What time she got up in the morning, what time she left home, what time she reached the railway station, what time the friends arrived, what time the train moved, what all stations it stopped at on way to Amritsar. Everything is being shared on WhatsApp. They reach Amritsar at 12:30 pm in the afternoon and take a cab to the hotel. They reach the hotel at around 1:00 pm and check in to their rooms and freshen up. Then they go for lunch at the hotel restaurant. During lunch they discuss the school politics, the management, and the new principal. After lunch, the women go back to one of the rooms and again go on a talking spree. After an hour of gossiping, discussing, and bitching about rest of the teacher friends, they decide to rest for some time and take short naps. Around 5:30 in the evening, Meenal wakes up the others and asks them to get ready as they have to visit the Golden Temple. The four friends take just 10 minutes to freshen up and then they leave for the gurudwara.

They take an auto-rickshaw and reach the gurudwara complex. It is that time of the evening when there is too much crowd and there is a big queue for the darshans. It takes them more than half an hour to get inside and seek the blessings of GURU GRANTH SAHIB. With dupattas on their heads and with folded hands, they kneel down and offer their prayers. Then they take a round of the platform where the holy book is kept and come out of the main hall. They take prasad from the bhaiji (a devotee from the gurudwara) and move towards the hall where LANGAR (free food from the God) is being served. The four friends eat the langar and then go around the gurudwara complex for a while, walking barefoot and experiencing bliss. From there they go to the nearby market and have some chaat pakora and chana kulcha. It is almost 8:00 pm when they decide to return to the hotel. They take an auto rickshaw and go back to the hotel and check into their respective rooms. Nobody feels like having dinner for they are already filled up with LANGAR prasad and chaat pakora.

Purvi and Taruna are sharing one room and Ekta and Meenal are sharing the other. Once inside their room, Purvi and Taruna freshen up, using the bathroom together. Then Purvi changes her clothes in front of Taruna. Taruna is looking at Purvi with amazement.

She sees Purvi daily in school, with full clothes on and finds her very sexy and delicious. Today she has the opportunity of seeing Purvi almost naked, with only her panties on. Purvi is an absolute delight without the clothes. She is tall and her long black hair is complementing her beauty. Taruna's eyes have just witnessed the most perfect curves and assets. Her skin is so smooth that it gives the feeling of a molten chocolate. Her aura is such that it is difficult for Taruna to set her eyes on one part of Purvi's body. Taruna is having all kinds of thoughts right now. she wants to reach out to Purvi and grab her in her arms. Purvi wears a short, netted black colour night gown which is looking too sexy on her. Taruna also changes and wears a nighty. She is constantly admiring Purvi and smiling. Purvi is enjoying the attention she has been getting from Taruna.

They come and sit on the bed when Meenal calls from the other room. Taruna picks the phone and from the other end Meenal asks if they would like to have some vodka. Taruna instantly says yes and asks Meenal to come to their room with the bottles. Taruna is delighted to hear that they are going to drink and enjoy. Meenal and Ekta have also changed to their night wear. They pick the glasses, the bottle and some wafers and go to Purvi's room. Purvi opens the door and lets them in. Taruna is in the bed, all excited on the prospect of getting drunk. Purvi, Meenal and Ekta sit on the bed, and the women get talking about hard drinks. Purvi says she loves drinking and can easily drink a quarter of a bottle. Taruna says even she can. Meenal is a bit shy talking about drinking habits, but says she will give them company. Ekta says two drinks is her limit. Purvi opens the bottle and makes drinks for the four of them. She likes to have vodka with Limca, so she tops up the four glasses with Limca and asks them to pick their glasses. The four of them pick their glasses, clink them, and say cheers.

The ladies are enjoying their drinks, and more than the drinks, they are enjoying all their womanly conversation. They are sharing their experiences on love, on love making, on their secret desires, and about the men in their lives. Each one of them has had a colourful past. Now Meenal and Ekta are happily (?) married and busy with whatever life has given them (no romance). Purvi is separated and is in a relationship with Vikram (though she is not telling them about him). Taruna's husband is working with some MNC abroad and does not come home for years, so she is staying with her in-laws and two kids (lonely soul). Life is really boring and dull and there is no fun (though right now she is enjoying and has some plans in her mind). They are sharing all kinds of stories, non-veg jokes, WhatsApp updates, X-rated movies and what not. Then they start clicking selfies and group photos, with vodka drinks in their hands. The bottle is almost empty and they are drunk. Meenal and Ekta say bye to Purvi and Taruna. Then they all hug and kiss each other for the longest of time and again they say bye to each other. After some confusion about who is going to sleep with whom, Meenal and Ekta finally go to their room.

Once Meenal and Ekta leave, Taruna sets her eyes on Purvi. Purvi is lying on the bed, her short see-through night gown exposing all her assets. Taruna is going wild and wants to pounce on Purvi, but then decides on going slow. She goes to Purvi's side, gets on the bed and very gently embraces Purvi. Purvi is drunk, half sleepy, tired, but in good mood. She does not realise that it is Taruna, her school colleague, a woman, who is hugging her. She also embraces Taruna. They stay that way for a while and then Taruna gets active. Her hands are running all over Purvi, feeling her everywhere. She first kisses Purvi on the cheeks, then her forehead, then again on her cheeks, and then on her lips. They are smooching and Taruna's hands are wandering and exploring all curves of Purvi. When Taruna tries to get more innovative, Purvi realises that this is not going in the right direction. She holds Taruna's hand and very gently asks her not to overdo it and just enjoy the kiss and hugs. Taruna is a bit disappointed but is still happy that she is getting to kiss and embrace Purvi, even if not getting to do one on one. The two women sleep naked that night, holding each other tightly in embrace.

The next morning when Taruna gets up, she sees Purvi in full daylight, all naked, lying next to her on the bed. The woman is so beautiful, she thinks.

Khoobsoorti pe teri, hairaan hain hum ....

Fida hain tujhpe, aur pareshaan hain hum....

Ji chahta hai, ki aaj kuchh kar jayen hum ....

Paake tujhe, tere aagosh mein mar jayen hum....

Last night, they were both drunk and Taruna did not get an opportunity to see Purvi naked (only felt her), but now, here she is, in full glory. Taruna immediately regrets not making out with Purvi yesterday night. But then she smiles, remembering what all she got to do with her. She could still feel her lips on her lips and her body mingled with hers. She could still smell the vanilla-like fumes rising from Purvi's body. She puts on her night gown and tries to wake up Purvi who seems to be in deep sleep. After a little effort, she is able to wake up Purvi, who immediately pulls over the bed sheet and covers herself, on finding herself full naked. Then she remembers what had happened the last night, and she looks at Taruna and smiles ....

Purvi asks Taruna to hand over a towel to her, as she has to go to the washroom. Taruna gives her the towel. Purvi covers herself up and goes towards the washroom. Taruna clicks some photographs of hers, with the towel barely covering her assets and showing off Purvi's broad shoulders and silky-smooth thighs. Taruna says she is looking too sexy in them. Purvi has a look at the pictures and finds them hot. She blushes and Taruna clicks her again. Purvi goes to the washroom, takes a shower and gets ready. They are going to the Wagah border today and in the evening, they have a train back to Delhi.

The four friends are having breakfast in the hotel restaurant and discussing about the fun they had last night. They are all giggling and blushing like teenage girls. Taruna shows them Purvi's pics which she had clicked in the morning and Meenal and Ekta are just blown away by her sensuousness. They say they have missed the opportunity. Taruna says better luck next time and they all laugh. Purvi asks Taruna to forward her the pics and as soon as she receives them in her mobile phone, she forwards them all to Vikram. Then she updates Vikram about what their itinerary is for today, that now they are going to the Wagah border, that they will be back on time for lunch, rest for some time and then leave for the railway station. The train to Delhi leaves at 4:30 pm and reaches New Delhi station at 10:00 pm. Purvi tells Vikram that she will reach home by 10:15 pm and he should come and see her at 10:45 pm. Then she types I love you and see you in the evening.

Its 8:30 in the morning and Vikram has just returned from the gym when he receives Purvi's messages. He opens the WhatsApp and sees Purvi's stunning, sexy, half nude pics. She is wrapped in a white mid-size towel which is covering her less and adding more sensuality to her already seductive frame. He goes through the messages and smiles. Then he replies with 'me too' and 'see you'.

Vikram meets Purvi in the evening, they discuss her trip and the wild encounter she had with Taruna. Vikram does not oppose her fondness for other women. He takes it lightly, thinking Purvi is just having fun and there is no serious side to her ventures.

THE OUTING

Life goes on and all is well between Purvia nd Vikram. They are meeting regularly at Purvi's house. Purvi is getting possessive of Vikram day by day and has full control over him. Whatever she says or asks of him is obediently followed by Vikram. The man has his own problems, but he never says no to Purvi. Most of the time, Purvi knows about whatever is going on in his life, and she also supports him fully. But when it comes to her own demands, she never compromises. She sees to it that he is connected to her emotionally, at all times. She loves him and does not want to lose him. He loves her and does not want to lose her. They go out for dinners, drives, movies and are inseparable. Purvi wants to spice up the relationship, but Vikram has his limits. He can do anything for her, but cannot marry her. Firstly, she is not divorced. Secondly, Vikram will not leave his children and wife. NOT EVEN FOR PURVI. He tries to keep her happy by all means, but she wants him fully. She wants him to leave his wife and kids and live with her, which is a very nice thought, but practically not applicable. Moreover, he had made it clear the first day: What Ramit has done to you, I will not do to Anjali.

Ananya, along with her job, has been preparing for MBA entrances exams. She sits for the online exam and gets a decent score. But decent is not good enough for pursuing MBA from a top-notch institute. She does not get any calls from top MBA institutions but manages to secure admission in two second-rung colleges. One is in Delhi and the other one is in Hyderabad. After a lot of thought and a lot of consultation with people who have knowledge of

MBA institutes, it is decided that she will go to Hyderabad. This institute is new in terms of campus and origin. Purvi asks Vikram to accompany her and Ananya to Hyderabad for the admission but Vikram very politely turns down the request, saying he has his limitations and it is not possible for him to leave the family and business and go with them (he does not want any eyebrows to be raised at home). He then asks Purvi and Ananya if they would like to celebrate and go for dinner with him (the three of them used to go for dinners occasionally). They both agree. Ananya is like a daughter to vikram. He has been supporting her and taking care of whatever she has asked from him (most of the time it is late night party permissions).

The night before Ananya is to leave for Hyderabad, Vikram takes her and Purvi out for dinner. Ananya loves parties and dinners, so is happy that Vikram uncle is taking them out. On the way, they talk all about the new life she is going to experience at the campus, the hardships of staying in the hostel, the new friends she is going to make, and of course, the studies. The studies are not to be compromised at all for anything. Whenever Vikram and Ananya are talking, Purvi is normally quiet. She likes Vikram being like a father figure and do all the talking. She feels more confident and comfortable when the kids mingle with him.

They go to a nice restaurant and the food choice is left for Ananya to decide. She wants to order some lobsters for everyone, which Purvi says she will not have because she does not like sea-food. So, Purvi and Vikram end up having their usual dal and Butter Chicken while Ananya experiments with the lobsters. After eating some, Ananya leaves it saying they do not serve good sea-food here and wishes to have some cold coffee. After dinner, Purvi and Vikram have some ice-cream and then they pay the bill and leave. On way back too, Vikram and Ananya are discussing her college. On reaching home, Purvi asks Vikram to come to her room for a while and then he can leave. Ananya knows that her mother and

Vikram uncle meet quite often. What she does not know is that they meet almost every third day. Vikram stays for a while and then goes home.

The next day, Purvi and Ananya leave for Hyderabad by air. They have made all the bookings in advance, like the air tickets, the hotel where they would be staying when the admission process is going on etc. It is going to be a two-day process. They reach the campus and after completing all the formalities like filling the various forms, paying of admission fees, taking the room in the hostel, and settling Ananya's luggage and other things in the room, Purvi and Ananya come back to the hotel. They have dinner together and before going to sleep, Purvi makes sure to update Vikram about the entire day's events. The next morning, Purvi and Ananya attend the orientation programme in the college and then Purvi goes to the hostel with Ananya. There she meets the girl who will be sharing the room with Ananya. Purvi makes sure that everything has been taken care of and she again checks the to-do list. Everything is fine. She stays with Ananya for a while, trying to explain various things to her and make her understand that these two years are the most important of her life and she should just concentrate on her studies and career. Then they have a very emotional see off, kissing each other, hugging each other, shedding some tears of joy, and finally saying bye and take care.

Purvi returns to her hotel and rests for some time as she has an evening flight back to Delhi. On reaching Delhi, she calls Vikram and asks him to come and meet her. Vikram asks her to rest as she must be tired of the journey and the hectic schedule she has had in Hyderabad, but she insists on him to come and meet her. Vikram gives in and goes and meets her in the night. They are together for good two hours, talking and sharing the details of her journey, the admission, the campus and then they talk about themselves. She hugs him and kisses him and does not want him to go back home.

Now that Ananya is gone, Purvi is going to be more demanding of Vikram, and demanding she gets. She wants him to spend more time with her, meet her every second day instead of meeting twice a week. Ananya is gone, Chhotu is busy with his studies, gym and his friends, daddy is busy watching television, resting and sleeping. After school, Purvi is alone most of the time. How much can she talk with Monisha and with Vikram over the phone? She wants somebody by her side, somebody she can love and talk to whenever she wants to; and that somebody has to be Vikram. But it is not possible. So, she has this feeling of emptiness. The feeling of not being desired. She wants to have that feeling of belonging, but Vikram does not belong to her. He belongs to her mentally, he belongs to her emotionally, he belongs to her by heart, but physically? Now, she wants him physically by her side all the time.

The relationship is getting dull, boring, and repetitive. It is the same thing every day. Talking, talking and talking. That too more about the daily chores. There is no romance left, and whatever romance they have in the bedroom, that too is getting dull, boring, and repetitive. Purvi wants action and action is missing. So, out of frustration, she starts arguing with Vikram on small and unimportant issues. Vikram always tries to handle the situation peacefully and patiently. Whenever Purvi is in a bad mood or is trying to argue or is in no mood of talking, he simply takes her in his arms, looks her in the eyes and smiles. She always melts on this gesture. She loves to be embraced by Vikram and then staying that way for 15-20 minutes. The hug is the strongest part of their relation. Thus, by avoiding the confrontations and their outcomes, Vikram is building a bridge of love. A bridge that is weak fundamentally and will collapse one day. AND COLLAPSE IT DOES. PIECE BY PIECE. His hugs, kisses, cuddles, embraces, I love you were not enough that day, which was to come next year and about which nobody knew nothing. Only the gods knew what they had in store for this man, a careless man. A GAAFIL.

THE THREAT

Purvi's father MR NAND KISHORE was at one point of time, a very RICH man. After getting his three daughters married (he had no son) he decided to wind up his business and live a peaceful, retired life. So, he sold his two factories and the two upper floors of his 500 square yards bungalow, while retaining the ground floor and the terrace rights of the second floor with himself. the entire money he got from the sales was converted into bank fixed deposits. The ground floor was more than enough for the husband and wife (wife is no more). Now, Purvi has been living on the same ground floor with them ever since she left her husband and came back to them. The two upper floors are occupied by MR ANAND (first floor) and MR GUPTA (second floor). Mr Gupta is a very arrogant, cunning and shrewd person. He has his eyes on the ground floor and on Purvi. He often visits MR Nand kishore and tells him that he has 40% rights in the ground floor. He makes sure that whenever he visits, Purvi is at home so that he can see her and derive pleasure from looking at her perfectly sculptured body. MR Nand kishore does not like MR Gupta and always feels threatened whenever he comes. Purvi is oblivious of his wandering eyes and always welcomes him as a family member.

One pleasant evening, MR Gupta comes to meets MR Nand Kishore. MR Nand kishore makes him sit in the drawing room and then calls Purvi and asks her to join them. MR Gupta is delighted to see Purvi. She is looking as good as always (sexy). MR Nand kishore asks MR Gupta the reason for his visit. MR Gupta starts by saying that the building is now too old (was built thirty-five years back) and requires to be demolished and built again. He says that he has talked to a builder friend of his and he is ready to construct a new house without charging them a single rupee. MR Nand kishore is amazed and says how is that possible and what will the builder get if he constructs the new house for free? MR Gupta says that the builder will make an extra floor in the building and keep that extra floor in lieu of the construction cost. Of course, the choice will be theirs and they will decide what floor to give to the builder, he adds.

MR Gupta knows that the man sitting across is old and weak and can be exploited very easily. He knows Purvi is a woman and will have no knowledge of building laws and can easily be fooled. So, to gain confidence and get a positive result from them, he makes sure that both father and daughter are involved. He knows that the final decision would be his, but he has to manipulate these people. MR Nand Kishore and Purvi know that their house is old and requires either a complete makeover or reconstruction.

MR Gupta has tweaked some points in the registry papers of the second floor which he had bought from MR Nand Kishore some twenty years back and shows them the clause which says that the owner of the second floor has 40% rights in the ground floor. MR Nand kishore is baffled by this seemingly-made error by his lawyer at the time of the sale of the second floor. He is a worried man. A small mistake made twenty years back is going to give him major problems. He asks MR Gupta for some time to think and says that they will let him know about their decision very soon. MR Gupta says they have a week to think about this and after that they should be mentally prepared to relinquish 40% of their rights in the ground floor to him.

After MR Gupta leaves, Purvi calls Vikram. She narrates the entire MR Gupta episode to him as it had happened, scene by scene. Vikram has a good knowledge of property papers because he himself is into construction. He knows all the basic points made in a registry and has a feeling that something is not right somewhere in their registry papers. He says he is coming to her house and that she should keep the copy of the registry papers handy.

In the meantime, Purvi informs her father that one of her friend's husband is a builder and she has had a talk with him. She says the friend's husband is coming over to their house to have a look at the papers and he will be advising them accordingly. Vikram reaches Purvi's house and parks his car just outside 112. Purvi has been waiting for him in the driveway and on seeing him, comes to the gate, smiles and takes him inside. She updates Vikram about what she has told her father about him (that he is her friend's husband) on the way to the drawing room. MR Nand kishore is already seated and he greets Vikram with a hello and Vikram also says hello to him.

THIS IS THE FIRST TIME VIKRAM IS SITTING FACE TO FACE WITH THE MAN WHO HAD REJECTED HIM AS A PROSPECT FOR HIS DAUGHTER.

This is the same man who had once come to his house and threatened his father with DIRE CONSEQUENCES if his son did not mend his ways and did not stop seeing his daughter. This is the same man who rejected him because he was not rich and did not match their status. This is the same man who had called him a ROMEO.

AND THIS IS THE SAME BOY (now a 48-year-old man) WHO HAS FORGIVEN HIM, BUT NOT FORGOTTEN HIM.

Now he is here to help because the old man is being threatened. He is the same boy who did not match their status then, but has set his own standards now. He is the same boy who was not welcomed into the family then, but is called for every little problem now.

Be-zari thee, toh paraya tha gaafil ....

Kisi ne saath, na nibhaya tha gaafil ....

Aaj baithe hain, ru-bru unke...

Jinhein waqt ne rulaya tha gaafil ....

Purvi shows the registry papers to Vikram and says that the lawyer who had drafted the document was a good friend of her father and he had full confidence in him. Vikram goes through the entire document and finds no fault in it. The only glitch is the language used. He assures Purvi and her father that MR Gupta can do no harm to them and cannot lay any claim to their property. He asks them to arrange a meeting with MR Gupta and says that he will also sit with them in the meeting. MR Nand kishore is relieved to hear that there is nothing wrong in the papers and that MR Gupta cannot claim that 40% in the property.

In the meantime, Purvi goes and makes tea for the three of them. She gets some biscuits along with the tea. Vikram loves tea and prefers to make it himself. He likes it strong. Purvi makes it very light with more milk in it. She looks at Vikram and smiles, and asks him to pick his cup. MR Nand kishore then asks Vikram if they should go for the collaboration with the builder. Vikram advises him that the house is in perfect condition and needed only some renovation. He also advises him on how to go about it.

Purvi had updated him with the details of the collaboration and Vikram had told her then that going for a collaboration was not a viable option. Right now, they had a complete driveway to themselves which they would lose if they plan to rebuild the house. The three servant quarters they have, will also go. Their rights to the terrace, will be relinquished. The front balcony and the backyard will be gone. They will lose all this and get a new floor, and the other two occupants of the upper floors, will lose nothing and yet get new floors. So, in the entire deal, she and her father were the losers and MR Gupta and MR Anand were the gainers.

A few days later, MR Gupta calls MR Nand kishore and asks what he has decided about the collaboration and if they can meet and discuss what the plans are. MR Nand kishore asks him to come around 7 pm in the evening and then asks Purvi to inform Vikram about the meeting. Purvi calls Vikram and informs him about the meeting. He says he will be there by 7 pm. Vikram reaches Purvi's house almost on time. She takes him to the drawing room where MR Nand kishore is already seated. Vikram sits on the sofa and says hello to him. He smiles and says hello. MR Nand kishore knows he has the right man to represent and defend them. He asks Vikram if he would like to have something. Vikram says no. The main door-bell rings and Purvi goes and opens the door. MR Gupta has come. Purvi brings him to the drawing room and asks him if he would like to have water or some tea. He says no, thank you and asks her to sit. Then he checks her out from head to toe. Vikram is watching this man and following his wandering eyes. He realises that the lustful eyes say that this man likes her and wants her.

MR Gupta looks at Vikram and is a bit taken aback by seeing a complete stranger sitting with MR Nand kishore. He asks MR Nand kishore who the person is. But before MR Nand kishore can reply, Vikram introduces himself and says he is his nephew. MR Gupta looks nervous and uncomfortable. He first looks at MR Nand kishore and then at Purvi. Purvi assures him that they can talk in front of Vikram, he is family. So, MR Gupta asks MR Nand kishore about his plans and his decision. MR Nand kishore says that they have not yet taken a final decision and are still considering his proposal. MR Gupta says that they should decide at the earliest or be ready to part with 40% of the ground floor. He tries to threaten them straight away.

Vikram has been watching this man for a while. He looks around 50, grey hair, tall and slim. He has this look of a typical businessman, which most property dealers have. The clothes he is wearing, tell the same story. So, the moment he says to MR Nand Kishore that he should be ready to part with 40% of the ground floor, Vikram interrupts and says, What 40% MR Gupta? You have no rights in the ground floor. The clause in the registry you are referring to says that in case of any natural calamity like earthquake, if the entire building comes down, and nothing remains of it except the rubble, only then you can claim 33% of the land. LAND - NOT THE GROUND FLOOR.

MR GUPTA is in a state of shock. He had not imagined that the man sitting across will have legal knowledge of the property documents and will oppose him. His plans are going for a toss. He is an angry man and stares at Vikram. Vikram is not intimidated and he looks back into his eyes conveying him the message .... Not to mess with me. MR Gupta gets up and asks MR Nand kishore to think about it once again, and that they can sit again and discuss, but now MR NAND KISHORE IS NEITHER AFRAID OF HIM, NOR INTERESTED IN HIS PROPOSAL. So, he simply nods in the negative. MR Gupta walks out of the drawing room murmuring some nonsense.

MR Nand kishore and Purvi are all smiles to have seen the agitated look on MR Gupta's face. They know the matter is over, once and for all and that MR. Gupta will not trouble them again. MR Nand kishore thanks Vikram, smiling and looking at him admiringly. Vikram is happy to see him smile and he himself smiles thinking that this man would have been his father-in-law if he had not made that mistake of choosing money over happiness.

MR NAND KISHOR ASKS VIKRAM IF HE WOULD LIKE TO HAVE A DRINK WITH HIM AND VIKRAM POLITELY SAYS

MAYBE SOME OTHER TIME. IT IS ANOTHER STORY THAT THE MAYBE SOME OTHER TIME NEVER COMES.

Purvi thanks Vikram in front of her father and follows him to the gate. There she commands him to meet her in the night. Vikram smiles and leaves. They meet in the night.

CORBETT SOJOURN

Of late, Purvi has again been asking Vikram to take her on a holiday. Vikram says that if she wants to holiday with him, they have to go abroad. Here, in and around Delhi, it is too risky for them to be seen together. From time to time, somebody known to either of them had always appeared at places where they were least expected being seen together. That was always an awkward situation for both of them. But they have somehow survived till now, not bothering to take notice of such people and by leaving things to the Gods.

Purvi has been having mood swings for some time; every now and then she is upset. She says it is because of the age factor, the hormonal changes the body is going through; but Vikram knows that is not the reason. He understands everything but prefers to remain quiet. He knows that one good reason for the mood swings is the perception she has about her relation with him. He knows she has been discussing everything about him with Monisha on a daily basis. Now, this woman (MONISHA), who herself is having multiple affairs with different men, how can she counsel Purvi on a steady relationship? What does she know about LOVE? What does she know about Vikram? Maybe she is close to Purvi, but even that does not give her the rights of making Purvi believe in whatever she says. The IRONY is that Purvi believes and does exactly what is advised and told by Monisha.

A MAN IS NOT WON BY WHAT SOMEBODY ELSES MIND SAYS TO YOU, HE IS WON BY WHAT YOUR HEART SAYS TO YOU ....

But Vikram does not interfere with their proximity. He knows it is of no use. He knows it is better for him to not bring in the topic of Monisha. He knows Purvi will not listen anything against her. He has known Purvi for three decades now, and he thinks he knows her the best. But he will never say this to her. NEVER. Some things never change; they are in your genes. Your nature, your mindset, your language, the things that have been imbibed in you since your childhood. Purvi always had this habit of sharing her secrets with other people, it just depended what she was sharing with whom. Like with Vikram, she shared her sister's stories, but not about Monisha; and with Monisha she shared Vikram's story and maybe not about her sisters.

OR maybe she needed THAT someone, who would support her on that particular matter and give her that psychological edge she needed on the third person. But Vikram never complained. He did not complain because he was willingly giving her that edge. He behaves like a flatterer, always ready to make her happy. So much so, that he will say sorry even if he is not at fault. Purvi is a spoiled woman, spoiled by him, himself. She would never apologize for anything and would say: I am like this only. I will behave like this only. You have to take it all and love me for who I am.

She was not like this in the beginning. She was an all-giving woman. A woman who loved him unconditionally. But she has changed over the years. Over the years, Vikram is feeling and experiencing the changes, but is silent.

In July that year, Purvi says to Vikram that she is going for a holiday to Jim Corbett park with friends. Vikram asks her when she was going and with whom. She says she is going in the morning, the next day, but she does not reply about with whom she is going. Vikram knows all her female friends, Taruna, Mona, Ekta, Meenal and all. He takes all their names and keeps asking her. BUT SHE DOESN'T BUDGE AND DOESN'T REVEAL. Purvi is not confirming with whom she is going, and this is a matter of concern. Why is she hiding and what is she hiding? Why couldn't she tell? Was she going with some MALE friend? SHE USED TO SAY SHE HAD SO MANY ADMIRERS. Vikram is upset but does not say anything.

Next morning, she leaves for Jim Corbett ....

EPICTETUS WAS A GREAT GREEK PHILOSOPHER WHO ONCE SAID: PEOPLE ARE NOT DISTURBED BY THINGS, BUT BY THE VIEW THEY TAKE OF THEM.

Vikram is obviously disturbed. His mind is disturbed, it is illusioned ....is she alone or with somebody? Is that a man or a woman? Who is this somebody? What if something goes wrong with her? What if something bad happens to her? What is she doing in Jim Corbett? Is she enjoying with the guy? Is she having sex with the guy?

He definitely knew that she was not with some woman friend, and he was sure she was not alone. She was not the lonely types. A woman who is on phone for 16 hours a day, cannot go alone anywhere; and Jim Corbett is too lonely a place in itself. He was sure that she was having a time of her life. She was always very interested in sex and Vikram knew that she could go out with somebody. She had once gone with MR DHAM, only it did not work out that time. A WOMAN WHO CAN GO OUT ONCE CAN GO OUT AGAIN. And she was not happy with Vikram. This was a good excuse to break free and go and enjoy life.

FOR FOUR DAYS VIKRAM WAS IN MENTAL TORTURE.

He called Purvi but she did not pick the phone. He messaged her and she did not reply. He received just two messages from her in four days. The first message was on the day she had left for Jim Corbett. It stated: I am sorry. Vikram could not understand why she was saying sorry. The second message came on the third day, saying: The network here is very poor. So cannot talk and cannot message. He waited all day, for four days, for any message or call from her, but there were no calls and no messages. The fifth day, in the evening around 5 pm, she comes back and messages him: I am back. Vikram is in office and the moment he sees the message, he feels relieved that she is back safely. Vikram asks her about the trip and she says it was good. Then Vikram asks her to share the details of the trip and she says there is no story and nothing to share about. Now this was so different from her last trip to Amritsar the last year. That time she had shared all the details along with all the selfies, even the semi-nude ones. But this time she was saying there is no story.

Vikram had himself taken a few family trips in the last six years. There was not a moment from those trips, not a picture from those trips, not a detail of those trips, which was not shared with Purvi. There was not a day, not an hour when he did not talk to her or message her. And here, this woman had just taken a trip… WITH WHOM? ONLY GOD KNOWS. WHERE? ONLY SHE KNOWS. WHAT DID THEY DO? ONLY THEY WHO WERE WITH HER, KNOW.

AND WHAT ABOUT VIKRAM AND HIS LOVE AND HIS TRAUMA? ONLY VIKRAM KNOWS; FOR, IT WAS HIS BAGGAGE.

She said there was no story and nothing to tell. Five days, you are somewhere, alone or with somebody, and there is nothing to tell. Not even small things like what time you left, how you went, and when you reached. AND THE QUESTION REMAINED … why did she send that message the first day … THAT SHE WAS SORRY? Purvi had said sorry only once in these last six years, when she had torn Vikram's shirt and he had left in anger. After that, she made sure it was Vikram who would say sorry for everything and not her. Then why did she say sorry ….?

VIKRAM SHOULD HAVE BEEN STRONG AND SHOULD HAVE SAID THE FINAL SAYONARA. THIS WAS ONE INCIDENT THAT HE SHOULD NOT HAVE IGNORED. BUT ....

Be-rukhi pe teri, pareshaan hoon mein ....

Be-wafai pe gaafil, pashemaan hoon mein...

Be-muravvat hai tu, janta hoon lekin ....

haarta hoon dil se, hairaan hoon mein ...

BUT THIS IS VIKRAM, A MAN WHO KEEPS HIS PROMISES. A MAN OF HIS WORDS. HOW CAN HE LEAVE HER? HOW CAN HE TELL HER THAT YOU ARE A CHEATER? HOW CAN HE BACK OUT OF THIS RELATIONSHIP AFTER ALMOST SIX YEARS? A FEW MORE DAYS, AND IT WILL BE SIX YEARS OF BEING TOGETHER AGAIN. NEXT MONTH IT WILL BE THIRTY-ONE YEARS SINCE THE BEGINNING OF THEIR STORY.

He could not leave her because of some whims of his, for he might even be wrong. Maybe she is going through a bad phase and will tell him in a day or two. Last time also she told him about Mr. Dham the next day. May be, this time too she will tell.

But this time, it was not to be told. This time there was no story to be told. This time there will be no next day or next few days. Vikram will forget after two days and they will move ahead just like the last time. Did he forget the Dham story? No. Will he forget the Jim Corbett trip? No. He will not forget. These things will remain somewhere in the back of his mind and will come out only when the time comes. When the downside in the story comes. And that time was not too far. That disaster was bound to happen and had already been scripted. IT COULD NOT BE AVERTED. But Vikram was unaware. He was a Careless Man. A Gaafil.

He just could not foresee what was to come. He believed in his love story and he believed in it too much. But the GAAFIL did not know, that sometimes, heroes are turned into villains and the story has a dramatic end rather than a happy ending.

THE RUNAWAY CHILD

Purvi's son Chhotu ... now, this is one over-confident, over-smart, but a confused character. Purvi has been after his life all the time and has been complaining for the longest of times. Since he is the only son, and close to Purvi, she wants him to just concentrate on his studies and career. She says that all the children in the family (her two elder sisters' kids) are well settled, so should be her daughter and son. Seema's elder son is into aviation and younger one is a tax consultant. Anita's son is an engineer and her daughter is working for a multinational. So Purvi wants both her kids to do better (professionally and in life) than her two sisters' kids. Chhotu had got admission into a Delhi college last year, but he withdrew his admission because the college was a bit far from his house. Then he opted for a private university and after paying the fees for the full semester (which was only Rs. 1.5 lakh) stopped going there after a few months, for now he wants to be a lawyer. So, he drops out and starts preparing for CLAT. He somehow manages to clear the exam and gets admission in a third rung law college in Bangalore.

Purvi again wants Vikram to go with her for Chhotu's admission as she had asked him in Ananya's case. Again, Vikram very politely says no, as he had said in Ananya's case. This time too, Purvi goes alone (accompanying Chhotu). She goes to Bangalore, settles Chhotu there and comes back. Now both the kids are studying out of Delhi and Purvi is staying with her father. She starts feeling lonelier. She is busier than ever with the phone now. Previously, Purvi's calls would be limited to school, Monisha and Vikram. After Ananya left home, Purvi's call-list included Ananya as well. Now, she had to add one more name to that list – Chhotu. There were many other people who Purvi considered important in her life, but they were not mentioned or discussed in her conversations. Now that both the kids had gone and daddy, an old man (busy in his own world), Purvi's work load was less and free time was in abundance. Vikram was trying to keep her happy by speaking to her whenever she called. However busy he might be, but he would take the call and speak till the time she hung up. As usual, he used to meet her after every two-three days, but tried to go as often as she asked him to, just so that she would not feel sad and lonely. Speaking more and meeting more often, did improve the relationship for some time. There were no more fights and arguments for some time and Vikram forgot about the Corbett episode. All he cared about was that he loved her.

In the first year itself, Ananya had made a few boy-friends in college which she did not tell her mother about. The girl never had good rapport with her mom; and, it was not her fault. She behaved like any teenager would at this age. Her mom just did not understand this simple logic according to her. According to the mother, the girl was just not to be trusted. She was spoilt and SHE WAS A BIG LIAR. Purvi keeps a close watch on her two kids, so tries to remain in maximum touch with them on phone, asking what time they get up, what's the breakfast time, what time they attend classes, what time they come back to their respective rooms, dinner time, sleeping time. ALL THE TIME.

Ananya's college and hostel are at a distance and both are out of the city. The students are allowed to go to the city only on Sundays for their shopping or enjoyments like movies or lunches and dinners at cafes. One Sunday, Ananya gets back to the hostel very late and gets a warning from the hostel warden. The parents are not informed because such incidents are normal and do happen in the hostels every once in a while. Moreover, she was not alone and there were three more students who had turned up late. So, they are given a warning and let off. Had the authorities not taken such incidents lightly, the bigger incident would not have happened. The next time, Ananya, along with a boy-friend of hers, just vanishes from college.

Purvi receives a phone call from a college official asking her to come to Hyderabad and take her daughter back. He says that the college is expelling ANANYA from the college for flouting serious college rules. The college official informs Purvi that her daughter had disappeared from the campus and was untraceable for four days. He says this was not tolerable and acceptable and will set a wrong precedent if not dealt strictly. So, they are expelling Ananya and the boy she had fled with.

What could Purvi say or answer to the college official? She knows her daughter is wrong. She has been like this forever. So, to save ANANYA'S future and career, Purvi pleads with him to let her daughter finish college as this was the final semester and her life and career were at stake. The official is a kind-hearted man and replies that he will speak to his seniors and try to help her.

Purvi calls Vikram and narrates the entire story and the conversation she had with the college official. She is angry, she is in tears, and she is all broken. Vikram tries to console her and says that everything will be fine; just believe in God and have patience. He goes and meets her in the night and stays with her for a while giving her much needed guidance, assurance and love.

The next day, Purvi calls the college official and asks about the status of Ananya's case. The official says that the college authorities are very much concerned about the two students' future and do not want to destroy their careers. But if they let them go unpunished, it will be a wrong example. PURVI pleads with him and as guided by Vikram says that she is a single mother and things are already difficult for her. She says she is ready to take all responsibility of her child and will apologise on Ananya's behalf. The official is convinced and ready to help. He asks Purvi to mail an apology letter to the head of the concerned department, apologising and taking full responsibility of what has happened and assuring that this will not happen again.

PURVI THANKS THE COLLEGE OFFICIAL FOR HIS HELP AND MAILS THE APOLOGY LETTER. ANANYA IS NOT EXPELLED.

Ananya is back home for holidays, and so is Chhotu. The family is in a state of great disturbance because of ANANYA'S latest misadventure. Purvi, Ananya and Chhotu have a serious argument over her ACCOMPLISHMENT. So much so that Chhotu, who is five years younger to Ananya, asks her: Did you use protection or not? Don't tell us you are getting pregnant. Purvi too joins her son and uses all kinds of expletives. She then calls Vikram and asks him to come and join the family discussion and counsel Ananya. She wants him to sit with them when they finally ask Ananya to either mend her ways or there is no place for her in the family.

Vikram does not want to join this family drama. He knows them all too well. He knows he is an outsider and Ananya will not take kindly to his interference. He knows Chhotu is a confused soul and has no brains of his own. He knows Purvi is upset right now but will be fine in a few days. BUT HE CANNOT SAY NO TO PURVI.

Vikram goes to Purvi's house and they all sit in the drawing room. Mr Nand kishore is also there but the old man is short of breath and short of words. On seeing Vikram, Ananya is uncomfortable and says she does not want to talk in his presence. Purvi is adamant and says that Vikram knows everything and will sit with them. The mother and son start shouting at Ananya and have a heated argument with her over the issue of her disappearing from college campus with an unknown boy. Chhotu gets hyper and says to Ananya that what she is doing is wrong and repeats the 'getting pregnant and using protection' sentence. Ananya loses her cool and shoots back that she is a grown-up girl and knows what is right and what is wrong. She asks both her mom and brother to shut up. Vikram is sitting tightly and watching everybody yelling at each other. He looks at MR Nand Kishore who is sitting across like a defeated man, watching the family circus like a muted audience.

Vikram is not liking these over-dramatic performances by Purvi, Ananya and Chhotu. What the three are yelling at each other is not in good taste, and he does not want to be a part of this milieu. They look like a family who has lost all love and all respect for each other. Just as he is thinking of getting up and going out of the drawing room, Purvi calls out to him and asks him to interfere. Vikram does not want to, but seeing all the drama, he just wants to convey a message to Ananya that would make her understand the family values and not that she is wrong and will not be tolerated.

He starts speaking: ANANYA, YOU ARE LIKE MY DAUGHTER, AND THIS IS NOT THE FIRST TIME ...... Just as he says these words and ANANYA cuts him short, snapping at him: HOW DARE YOU UNCLE! YOU ARE SO CHEAP!

Vikram is stumped. He did not expect her to disrespect him and be rude with him. Moreover, this choice of words by her was a complete bouncer. Nobody had dared to use these kinds of words to him in his everlasting memory. This girl has just shattered his self-image, and destroyed his self-respect.

A girl who can call her mother A BITCH will have no respect for anybody. He couldn't imagine how Purvi had thought that she will respect Vikram and will listen to him.

As if this was not enough, Vikram is bowled over by another googly, this time by the confused and lost soul ... Chhotu. He changes sides and defends his sister by saying that he (Vikram) has no right to interfere and cannot talk to his sister like that. Vikram wonders ...like what? He had not even completed the sentence and was stopped by Ananya, and now this boy is defending his sister. The brother who was asking his sister to use condoms and not get pregnant just two minutes back, is now supporting her (out of brotherly love or a sudden change of heart, God only knows).

WHAT IS THIS ... SOME KIND OF PSYCHO FAMILY SUPPORTING EACH OTHER WHEN AN OUTSIDER INTERVENES?!

Vikram just wants to leave and is about to get up again when Purvi sees the displeasure and disappointment on his face and shouts at her two children: He can talk to you any which way he likes. I have called him here. BUT THE DAMAGE HAD ALREADY BEEN DONE. Vikram gets up to go and before walking out of the room, looks at Ananya and Chhotu and says to them both: if it were Ayaan and Aryan instead of you, and if they had spoken like you just have, I would have given one tight slap on their faces each.

SAYING THIS, HE WALKS OUT OF THE DRAWING ROOM. Purvi follows him to the gate and tries to pacify him. She says she is sorry for what has happened. The look on her face says she is really sorry. Vikram gives her a smile and walks to his car.

He sits in the car and drives away. He is still in a state of shock and analysing the entire ten minutes he was there in the drawing room. What a shame this was! Disgusting! Was this what he had come here for? To get insulted? The focus had shifted from Ananya's sex escapades to Vikram's interference. The girl had run away from college with her boy-friend. She was untraceable for a few days. The brother is asking her whether she took precautions or not and there is no response or objection to that. But the moment he (Vikram) opened his mouth, all hell broke loose. The girl went wild and got abusive. There were no answers to where she was for four days and with whom and what were they doing wherever they had gone to. She was behaving as if they had been singing duets and dancing in the rain, just like it happens in the movies.

NOT ONCE DID IT OCCUR TO HIM THAT THIS WAS JUST A REPEAT OF PURVI'S ESCAPE TO CORBETT.... LIKE MOTHER, LIKE DAUGHTER?

On the way home, Vikram stops at a 24/7 convenience store to buy a packet of cigarettes and cold coffee. Purvi calls and he says he will talk to her later. He is in no mood to talk to anybody right now. He sits in the car, lights a cigarette, and takes a drag. Then he picks up his phone, opens the contacts list, and blocks Ananya's number. He doesn't want to talk to this girl ever again, no matter what. Not knowing, that the girl he is blocking right now, will almost a year later, block him from meeting her mother and try to get him LOCKED-UP. Not knowing, that the girl he doesn't want to talk to right now, will make sure that everybody in the police station listens to her and not him, a year from now. Not knowing, that the girl he always helped and supported, will make sure that no help or support is available to him when she retaliates.

Be-khabar hai tu, tujhe apni khabar nahin ...

Be-kadar hai tu, tujhe apni kadar nahin ....

kuchh le khabar apni, kuchh kar kadar gaafil ....

Mushkil badi hai aage, aasaan safar nahin ....

Vikram is very fond of music, so he turns on the music in the car. 'Love is stranger than fiction' is playing on the system and Vikram falls in love with the words .... When the tables turned, it's like a religion, where the hearts concerned, it's like an addiction, in a brave new world, love is stranger than fiction. Vikram smiles to himself. This is what love does to you .... You are insulted and you still keep smiling.

THE POWER OF THE WILL

A few months later, Purvi asks her father to draft a WILL in her favour, giving nothing to the two elder sisters. MR Nand Kishore has not been keeping well off late, and age is another factor (he is 80) she has kept in mind. So, she wants all things to be taken care of in time, just in case anything serious happens to him. Moreover, the sisters are not to be trusted. Both of them have an eye for all things belonging to MR Nand kishore. So, she wants everything to be put on paper (WILL) in detail.

MR Nand kishore has been a good father to his three daughters and loves them equally. He has his sympathies and emotions for Purvi as she has been separated from her husband and raising her two kids on her own and has been living with him for long and taking care of him. But still, he wants to give Anita and Seema some money and some portion of his property (the terrace maybe). So, he tries to convince Purvi that after he is gone, the two sisters will be the ones who will BE THERE for her; they will love her and take care of her. So, she should respect them and respect the relation they share. But Purvi is adamant and says that she does not want to keep any relation with the two of them and will not be giving a single penny to her sisters from her father's money. She says they are already too well off and it will not matter to them if they don't get anything.

MR NAND KISHORE IS LEFT WITH NO CHOICE BUT TO IGNORE HIS TWO ELDER DAUGHTERS IN THE WILL.

Purvi knew that Anita was a nominee in some of the FDs (FIXED DEPOSITS) that Daddy had in his name. So, she convinces him and gets the FDs cancelled and gets all the money transferred to her own account, apart from making new FDs in her name. Next, she gets the WILL drafted and asks daddy to appoint Vikram as the EXECUTIONER to the will. MR Nand kishore also knows that Vikram is one person who can be trusted and who will be there whenever needed as he had proved in Mr Gupta's case. So, Purvi calls Vikram and asks him to WhatsApp his Aadhar card number as she needs it for the WILL. Vikram obliges. The will is made and registered.

MR NAND KISHOR IS THE TESTATOR, VIKRAM IS AN EXECUTIONER AND PURVI A LEGATEE.

Neither Vikram asks, nor Purvi shares the exact content of the will. Vikram knows that the will completely favours Purvi and that it has nothing for the two sisters in it. But he also knows that the sisters are really well off and the terrace rights will not make them any richer. He knows that MORALLY and ETHICALLY the WILL is wrong. It has been manipulated. He knows that the FATHER has been manipulated and brainwashed. That the father wanted to give the other two daughters something out of love, with free will. He also should have. But, Vikram has no say in these matters and moreover, he does not want to involve himself in these family matters of hers, anymore. Last time (when Ananya was rude to him), it was a very embarrassing situation, and he does not want a repeat of that.

SO, VIKRAM CHOOSES TO BE KIND RATHER THAN BEING RIGHT. AS FOR PURVI … EVERYTHING IS FAIR IN LOVE AND WAR; AND SHE IS READY FOR A WAR WITH HER TWO SISTERS.

Ananya is coming for Diwali holidays and Purvi has to pick her from the airport. She calls Vikram and asks him to accompany her to the airport at around 1:00 am in the night. She says she will pick him from outside his house at 12:30 am and will drop him after picking Ananya. Vikram is fine with it. This is not the first time he is going to pick Ananya; he has accompanied Purvi many a times and many a times he has also gone alone. But this is the first time after that argument with Ananya. Still Vikram is fine with it. He loves Purvi and this is one way of showing his affection and respect for her. To the extent that even his self-respect does not matter where he has to stand with her or for her.

Purvi picks Vikram at the exact time and they leave for the airport, only that Purvi has switched her seat and Vikram is driving. They reach the airport at 1:05 am and are in the parking area when Purvi gets a message on her phone that the flight is delayed by almost an hour. They sit in the car, waiting, talking, smiling at each other, holding each other's hand and in between, Purvi resting her head on Vikram's shoulder. At 2:15 am, Ananya calls and says that she is standing outside the airport gate no. 3, and they go and pick her up. She sits in the car and Purvi asks her to say hello to uncle, which Vikram never wanted Purvi to do. Ananya says hello and Vikram replies with a hello. The entire way back, mother and daughter are talking so normally and smilingly, as if nothing had happened between them, and Vikram is driving silently as if he is a hired driver. Vikram stops the car near his house and gets down. Purvi comes to the driver's seat, says thank-you and bye to Vikram and drives away. It's 3 am and Vikram is wondering … would he have started talking to Ananya if he was in Purvi's place …. or Purvi not talking if she was in his place. He smiles… it's a strange world. He goes home and sleeps.

THE MAKEOVER

It's almost year end and Purvi wants the house to be renovated. She has approached a few interior designers and architects, none of whom is giving her a clear picture regarding the work they will be doing and the kind of money they would be charging. They are all confusing her by not quoting a certain amount for a certain work. Though money is not a problem because daddy has agreed to spend as much as she wants, Purvi still wants to spend it wisely. The only thing is to get a good contractor, who can take the job and deliver within a time-frame with the best of quality and best of designs.

Ananya will complete her management studies the next year and Purvi wants to marry her off as soon as she gets a good job. So, she wants the work to start immediately and finish it as soon as possible. She calls Vikram and asks him to come home to discuss the designs, the work, and the costing with her and daddy.

Vikram is sitting with Purvi and her daddy and they are discussing how to get the work done. Vikram says that the house is in perfect condition and that it only requires a paint job and some new furniture and furnishings, to which daddy agrees but Purvi disagrees. SHE WANTS A COMPLETE MAKEOVER. Then Vikram suggests that it would be easier to get the work done themselves by hiring different people for different jobs and not giving all the work to one contractor. That way it will be cost effective and they will not be depending on one person alone. MR Nand kishore likes the idea and agrees with Vikram; but Purvi is not concerned about money when it comes to her house . Moreover, she does not want to take the responsibility of running around the labour guys. She wants to give all the responsibility to an architect or an interior designer and let him handle the job, solely. So finally, they all agree on giving the job to an architect or an interior designer.

The next topic of discussion is whether to shift to a rented accommodation or shift to the back portion of the house and get the work done. Vikram says that keeping her daddy's health in mind, they should shift to some small flat and hand over the entire house to the architect. That way, daddy's health will not be compromised and the architect will also get a free hand and work in all the rooms can be started at one go. He says that because the kids are studying outstation and she herself will be at school for half of the day, they can easily manage with a two-room flat. Purvi says that this they will decide once the work is allotted to an architect. Then she asks him if he knows any interior designer or an architect. Vikram knows a lot of people and can get the work done easily and on reasonable budget, but he does not want to get involved in anything that can be problematic tomorrow. HE KNOWS PURVI IS VERY FUSSY ABOUT GETTING THINGS DONE HER WAY and he will be spoiling his relation with her if he gets involved. So, he says no to her and stays away from this project.

After a few days, the renovation work is given to some interior designer who is a friend of the uniform supplier's son from Purvi's school. The interior designer's name is Monika and the school uniform supplier's son's name is Prakash. Now this man named Prakash is Purvi's friend and Vikram doesn't know anything about him. Monika visits Purvi's house and inspects what all work has to be done and accordingly gives her an estimate of the money she would be charging.

Purvi calls Vikram and asks him to come to discuss this estimate given to her, in Monika's presence. In the evening, Monika, her assistant John, Purvi and her father, are all sitting in the drawing room, discussing the work to be done and the money she is charging. Vikram enters the drawing room and sits on a chair. He sees Monika and John and has a gut feeling that these guys are AMATEURS and IMMATURE and look like FRAUDS. They don't look like professionals and they will be giving Purvi a lot of problems. But he does not want to interfere. He has seen the results of interfering in this family's affairs.

ONCE BITTEN TWICE SHY. So, he prefers to remain silent this one time, not knowing that he should have spoken up. Spoken up, that these people should not be given the contract, that they don't deserve it. But how can he speak? How can destiny allow him to speak? For these very people have to be responsible for his final break up with PURVI in the next few months. The countdown has started and the process of their getting separated the second time has begun. THE CONTRACT IS GIVEN TO MONIKA ON PRAKASH'S RECOMMENDATION AND RS THREE LAKH GIVEN AS ADVANCE.

The next few days Purvi is busy getting things shifted from the first room and the drawing-dining to the two bedrooms in the back portion of the house. She has declined Vikram's suggestion of living in a separate house. The servant quarter is converted into a temporary kitchen and the dismantling work in the front portion of the house starts. Things to be replaced and the things no longer required are sold off to a local scrap dealer. Vikram and Purvi are not meeting in the nights anymore. The first room is under renovation and meeting in the back room is not possible because the two back rooms are next to each other and PURVI doesn't want to disturb daddy or want him to know that she has been meeting Vikram secretly. BUT THEY ARE IN REGULAR TOUCH OVER THE PHONE.

2020

It is a new year with a lot of new hopes and new beginnings, but MR Nand Kishore has not been keeping well. Purvi is busy on three fronts now ... daddy's health, the school and the renovation of the house. She takes daddy to Apollo Hospital and the health check-up reveals that he has lung cancer. The doctors advise some medicines instead of chemotherapy, keeping his age and health in mind. This news upsets Purvi; she is not ready for this. Already she is going through a lot of mental stress because of her tight schedule and never-ending jobs like managing the school work after school, preparing breakfast, lunch, and dinner for herself and daddy, constantly watching the labour working in the front portion, and arranging whatever they are asking for. AND NOW THIS CANCER NEWS. She starts having mood swings on a daily basis and gets irritated on every little thing. She is arguing and fighting with Vikram every second day. He understands her situation and handles himself well, keeping himself away from getting into any conflict with her.

Vikram had forgiven MR Nand kishore for what he had said and done to him thirty-two years back, the day they sat together and had a cup of tea (while resolving the issue of MR GUPTA'S threats over the property rights). Now Vikram wants to meet him and wish him well. So, he asks Purvi if he can come and meet him, and Purvi very rudely says no. She says she has no time for him and his courtesies. Vikram feels bad but does not say anything. NEXT TIME WHEN PURVI CALLS, SHE SAYS SHE IS SORRY FOR HER

BEHAVIOUR. But this is GAAFIL ...a careless man. he does not mind anything that Purvi says.

Izzat na karo na sahi, be-izzat na karo gaafil ....

be-murawwat ho tum, hum be-gairat nahin ....

In early March, some Coronavirus news starts spreading across the globe. The media says it is a pandemic which is going to wreak havoc in the world. It has originated in WUHAN (CHINA), killing thousands of people in a few days. In EUROPE and the US, people have started getting infected, but not many cases have been reported in INDIA as yet. People, of course, are scared and have started taking counter-measures like not stepping out of their houses, not going to parties or big gatherings or family functions, and storing essentials for months ahead just in case it gets dangerous and ugly. Ananya and Chhotu are back home as there is news that the world is going for a total shutdown.

On March 22nd, the PRIME MINISTER of India announces a complete lockdown for forty days, starting that day itself. There is no way to fight this pandemic and the only way to remain safe is to be contactless. So, nobody is allowed to venture out of their houses. The police and the para-military are deployed to maintain law & order and make sure that this lockdown is followed strictly. All offices, markets, schools, universities, cinema halls, gyms ... everything except the hospitals, medicine shops and essentials shops are closed for indefinite time. People are allowed to go out only to buy essentials, from 9 am to 5 pm. After that, it is a curfew like situation.

Fourth day into the lockdown, when the entire INDIA is locked in their homes, Purvi calls Vikram and asks him to come and meet her in the night. She says, the kids will be sleeping with daddy, and she will be alone in her room, so it is safe for them to meet. Vikram is happy that Purvi is inviting him home as it has been more than a month since they had last met. This was the longest gap between their meetings as they normally met every second or third day. These are not normal times. This is a time when the entire world is living in fear. These are the times when people of any one family are trying to maintain distance even from each other. These are the times when nobody wants to be a guest and nobody wants to be a host. And here, Purvi has invited Vikram and he is more than willing to go. This is love.

At around 10:30 pm, he leaves for Purvi's house. The roads are all empty and deserted. He is just out of his block and he sees a police barrier put up on the main road. He reaches the barrier and is stopped by a policeman. The policeman in a very strict tone, asks him where he is headed to at this hour and doesn't he know that nobody is allowed to venture out after 5:00 in the evening? Vikram says that one of his friend's father is not well and he is going to see him but the policeman is not amused to hear the reason. He warns Vikram that his car will be impounded and he will be arrested if he does not comply with government orders. He asks Vikram to take a U-turn from there and return home. Vikram takes a U-turn, drives on the wrong side of the road and goes back home. He parks the car outside his house and calls Purvi. He narrates her the entire conversation he has just had with the policeman. Purvi is very disappointed and says that whenever she wants to meet him, there is always some or the other problem. She says that today it was a perfect opportunity for them to meet and it did not happen. Vikram assures her that he will meet her very soon.

March goes by. The lockdown is being followed seriously. Purvi and Vikram have not yet met. Vikram is spending time watching lot of television and helping Anjali with the household chores. Purvi is busy taking care of daddy and the kids and most of her day is spent in the makeshift kitchen (servant quarter) preparing meals.

One morning in the first week of APRIL, Vikram goes to a store to buy some essentials. There is a long queue and the waiting period is almost one hour. Vikram calls Purvi from there and asks if she requires anything. She gives him a list of a few things and asks him if he can come and deliver. She knows there are long queues and it is tiring to arrange or buy things in the lockdown. Then there is this problem of not being allowed to enter or exit colonies without the identity proofs. But Vikram assures her that he will come and deliver the things she has asked for. He buys all the things that are on the list given to him by his wife and the ones sent to him by Purvi on WhatsApp. Thereafter, he starts for Purvi's house. On the way, he is stopped at a police barrier and asked the reason for moving out and to show his identity proof. He shows his ID card and says he is returning home after buying the essentials. He even shows them the bag containing all the stuff and they allow him to proceed.

Vikram reaches Purvi's house and parks the car across the road. He calls her to say that he has reached and she asks him to come to the makeshift kitchen. Vikram opens the gate and walks through the driveway to the kitchen. Purvi has a big smile on her face when she sees Vikram. She asks him to wash his hands and then remove his mask (it is mandatory to wear one when going out) and wash his face. Vikram smilingly does what he is told to do. Then he gives her the things she had asked him to buy for her. They are both looking at each other and smiling. Vikram opens his arms SHAHRUKH KHAN STYLE and Purvi hugs him. It has been a long time since they have hugged each other. They stay like that for a while and then they both decide that till the lockdown is in force, they will meet in the kitchen and only in the afternoons. Vikram stays with her for another half an hour and then leaves for home.

Now this going out for buying essentials is a wonderful and successful idea and it has already worked. Whenever Purvi wants to meet Vikram, she informs him in advance that at this particular time, I will be free and daddy or the kids will not be coming to the kitchen. It is normally around 1 pm in the afternoon. At this time, the kids are sleeping (after watching TV the whole night) and daddy is in the puja room. Vikram too makes sure that he moves out of his house much before the given time and is through with buying essentials in time and reaches Purvi's place on time. They are spending some quality time together. The kitchen is like a honeymoon suite for them.

The lockdown is eased in early May. Offices and local markets are allowed to open from 10 am to 6 pm. Since the entire nation was on a stand still mode for more than a month now, the government wants things to start getting normal and the economy to move forward. Vikram had been working from home all this while, doing household work and office work. So, it is a bit of a relief as he starts going to office. He and Purvi had been meeting in the afternoons and these meetings happened only when Purvi wanted them to happen. Now it is not possible for Vikram to meet her in the afternoons, so one day, after office, at around 7 pm, he goes to meet Purvi. She is in the kitchen and preparing dinner. He goes and knocks on the glass door of the kitchen. She was not expecting him, so is surprised to see him. She opens the door and asks how he had come. He says he was missing her so thought of surprising her. She says he should have called before coming and that she does not want her children to know that he is coming and meeting her. Vikram feels bad about what she has just said and picks his office bag and leaves. Later, over phone, Vikram says to Purvi that he will not come to meet her or talk to her unless she calls or she wants to meet. She calls him the next day and asks him to meet.

Vikram is in office and Purvi calls. She says that the renovation work has started again and she wants to meet him to discuss about the same. Vikram says that he will come and meet her after office hours. After office, Vikram goes and meets her and discusses the work in detail with her. The work is going on at a snail's pace and Purvi is not happy either with the raw material supplier or with the labour. Vikram says that he will talk to the tiles supplier and ask him to deliver the required tiles ASAP. He further suggests that she should talk to Monika and push her for getting the work finished as soon as possible. It has already been delayed by two months because of the lockdown. THE TILES SUPPLIER DELIVERS THE TILES THE VERY NEXT DAY. Vikram had called him. Purvi calls Vikram and thanks him.

Two days later, Purvi blocks Vikram's phone for almost three hours. When she unblocks and Vikram calls and enquires about why she had blocked him, she says she had gone to the doctor and did not want him to disturb her. Vikram cannot digest this stupid answer of hers. Anybody who is sensible enough, when told not to call during the doctor's appointment time, will never call. Her answer is too lame. He knows something is fishy but he does not say anything as he does not want to hurt himself.

A week later, they again have an argument. This time, they are sitting in the kitchen and Purvi says to Vikram that there is no romance left in their relationship. She says she had discussed this with Monisha and Monisha's take on the matter is that now they are more like husband and wife. Vikram is not surprised to hear Monisha's name; he knows Purvi has been sharing everything about him with her all these years. He is not bothered about Purvi sharing their personal details with Monisha. What he is surprised about is that even after seven years together, she is not talking to him openly about their relationship, but seeking somebody else's advice. This woman is looking for fake love instead of pure love. She says she does not want a second husband, but wants a boyfriend. Vikram is not happy to hear this husband-boyfriend story. He has tried to be a true person to her, with a truthful heart and truthful emotions. He has never faked himself. Now, it is up to her whether she wants to take him as a husband or a boyfriend.

Also, as far as her asking him to be a boyfriend is concerned, she herself had acted more like a wife to him rather than a girlfriend. Purvi had always loved him and taken care of him like a good WIFE. She had loved him more in these seven years than his legal wife Anjali has in twenty-five years. Purvi had been a part of all the major personal and business decisions he had taken in these seven years. She had been the guiding force. She had taken care of his health and accompanied him to the doctors and hospitals whenever he was not well. She had improved his eating habits, his sleeping and resting patterns, his exercise and walk regimes and most importantly she had stood by him through thick and thin. Always encouraging him to live a wonderful life and fulfil whatever he desired of.

HE LOVES HER NOT BECAUSE HE LOVES HER, HE LOVES HER BECAUSE SHE WAS LOVINGLY LOVABLE. BUT SHE HAS CHANGED OVER THE YEARS....SHE REALLY HAS.

Just fifteen days back she had said that she was happy to be his second wife and that if Anjali was making him do all the hard work at home during lockdown and still not happy with him, she was more than willing to take him. Now this U-turn from what she herself had said was not making sense. After spending almost seven years like husband-wife, she wanted him to be a boyfriend. Maybe there was something that she wanted from him and was not getting. Or maybe it was the LOCKDOWN EFFECT. There was news in the media that the lockdown was having adverse effects on relationships. Couples were not able to handle this too much being together and were hence splitting. Whatever it was, it was not good ....

Now, how could he ask her not to take advise from others and just savour what THE GODS have given you as a gift ... the love of a person you want to be with? He knows she will not listen to him, for right now she is under the influence of what MONISHA THE MENTOR has told her. So, he just says that he is what he is and she replies that is not enough. Vikram does not like the way she has been talking, so he says bye and leaves. In the evening, he calls her and she disconnects the phone. Vikram does not like this disconnecting of phone by her and calls her again. She disconnects the call again. So, he messages her that he will be coming to meet her in the night at around 9 pm. He loves her and does not want to lose her and this woman has been taking him for granted for some time now. She talks when she wants to, she meets when she wants to, and still makes him feel guilty for what destiny has done to her life as if he is solely responsible for all the mess in her life.

Vikram goes to meet Purvi and Ananya is in the kitchen instead of her. Ananya refuses to open the door and says mom has asked her not to open the door and that she does not want to talk to you. Now, this girl and Vikram have not been talking for months now, and her telling Vikram that she will not open the door and that mom has asked her to do so, annoys Vikram. He asks her to tell her mom that things are over between him and her. The girl shows no emotions, and the look on her face tells a story that this is what they want. TO BREAK FREE ...

Purvi messages Vikram late in the night and says she wants to talk. Vikram asks her to call.

THAT NIGHT, PURVI CALLS VIKRAM AND SAYS THAT HE WILL NOT COME TO MEET HER UNLESS HE IS TOLD TO. NOT NOW AND NOT AFTER DADDY IS GONE. SHE SAYS SHE IS NOT A PLEASURE-GIVING MACHINE .... VIKRAM DOESN'T LIKE THE WAY SHE IS TALKING BUT ASSURES HER THAT HE WILL NOT VISIT HER AND NOT TALK TO HER.

In the first week of June, it is Purvi's birthday. Vikram and Purvi have not been talking and he does not wish to talk to her ever, but he does not want to spoil her birthday either. He wants things to end on a happy note. IN A CORDIAL WAY. In a way that if they ever cross each other's paths, there are no hard feelings. That they can see each other eye to eye, smile and say hello to each other. So, he decides that he will go one last time to her place, wish her, cut the cake and come back. END OF THE STORY.

So, on her birthday eve, Vikram buys a cake and goes to her house at around 10 in the night, to wish her. Purvi is in the kitchen and he knocks on the glass door. She sees him, gives a broad smile, and opens the door. Once inside, she hugs him very tightly, as if everything was normal between them and nothing had happened five days back. Vikram wishes her Happy Birthday and asks her to cut the cake. They share a piece of cake and then she gives a piece each to Ananya and Chhotu. The rest goes into the refrigerator. Purvi makes sure that Vikram stays with her for a while and leaves only when she allows him to; and that he does and does with a smile. He knows this is the last time he is meeting her, so he wants her to be happy. They are talking and she asks him if he will have dinner with her. He says he has already had. She asks if he would like to have something and he says he just had the cake. She says the cake is too yum and if he will like to have some more. He says he will. She opens the refrigerator and takes out two pieces, one for him and one for herself.

Vikram is relishing the Chocolate Truffle cake; it is his favourite. He likes it so much that he can eat an entire cake all alone. The conversation continues and he asks her why she had asked Ananya to lock the door and not open it for him when he had come the last time. Purvi is surprised and says she never asked Ananya to lock the door and will ask her why she did that. Still, Vikram could not make out that one of them was a liar and playing smart with him. How could he ... he loved this woman and when you are in love, you don't use your brains. Instead, you go by what your heart tells you. Purvi pampers him with all her love and they stay in the kitchen for an hour. By the time Vikram leaves, the thought of him leaving her, has left him.

THE FCUK UP

A few days later, Purvi calls Vikram and says she wants to meet him in the night. But this time they will not sit in the kitchen (it was getting risky as both Ananya and Chhotu kept sneaking around) but in the car. She asks him to get a black-colour film pasted on his car windows so that nobody can see them from outside. That way they will have privacy and will not be bothered by anybody. Vikram smiles at this idea of hers and says he has a pair of sun-shades and will put them on the car windows when he comes. She asks him to come prepared for the fun he is going to have and sends him some HOT videos on WhatsApp. Vikram just sees the content for a second and knows it is going to be one hell of a night. He knows she is going to get wild. BUT he also knows how to keep his cool and keep her in control. So, it is decided that they will sit in the car and meet at their usual time .... around 10:30 pm.

In the night, before leaving for Purvi's house, Vikram takes out the sun-shades from the car trunk and fixes them on the windows. He then checks from outside if anything can be seen inside. Nothing is visible. He smiles and gets into the car and drives towards Purvi's house. He parks the car across the road and calls Purvi. She asks him to wait in the car and says she will join him in two minutes. Vikram lights up a cigarette and takes a drag. He knows Purvi is very bold and adventurous, but this idea of getting the windows dark and then get a little HANKY PANKY in the car itself has taken him by surprise. These kinds of ideas never came to his mind. MAYBE HE IS NOT INNOVATIVE.

Purvi comes and sits in the car. She is wearing a short night dress which she normally wears while working in the kitchen. Vikram looks at her and smiles. She always looks beautiful and her face always glows when she has to meet him. He asks her what she has said to daddy or the kids and she says she has told Ananya that she is going for a drive with uncle. BUT THEY ARE NOT GOING ANYWHERE AND THE CAR IS PARKED RIGHT OUTSIDE HER HOUSE.

Now this is not the car (sedan) in which they normally used to go for drives and dinners, and could sit closely and comfortably in. This is a BIG SUV which is a delight to drive but is not lovers-friendly. Front seats are higher and much apart. So, it takes some effort to reach out to the person sitting next to you if you have to kiss him or hug him. This is what Purvi was not liking; she did not like the distance. So, she hops on to the back seat and then asks Vikram to get in the back seat as there it will be more comfortable to sit and hug and kiss. Vikram too jumps in the back and the two hug each other tightly. It's been just five minutes in the car's back seat and Vikram is already uncomfortable. Each time a vehicle passes them and the light from the headlight of that vehicle falls on them, Vikram has a feeling that maybe somebody is watching them. What if some cop is passing and he stops and sees them sitting in the car in a compromising situation? He asks Purvi to stop what she is doing and suggests that they should move to the kitchen. Purvi says it is ok here and that a lot of things happen here, at the same spot, in so many different cars. Nobody ever stops or objects. So, she suggests that they should continue .... but Vikram is adamant.

They leave the car and go to the kitchen. Purvi goes inside to inform Ananya that she and uncle are sitting in the kitchen and that nobody should disturb. She comes back and hugs Vikram. This is what she likes the most, and this is what Vikram loves the most. The hug is the most beautiful form of emotion according to both of them. They stay in the kitchen for an hour and then Vikram leaves. Things are not normal, but they look normal. Vikram has a very good habit of keeping things close to his heart. He does not let people know what kind of emotions he is going through or what he is feeling about them. He just wants everybody to be happy and keeping Purvi happy was his prime objective.

Three days later, Vikram is at home and watching television. Purvi calls him and asks him if he can come in the evening. He says if it is something important, he will come right away. She says it is about the renovation work. Monika has stopped the work and is asking for more money. So, she wants him to come and check the work done and then they can decide on what to do next. He says he will reach in half an hour.

Vikram goes to Purvi's house and sees the work and the quotation given by Monika. He, along with Purvi, measures the entire area which is under renovation and in detail works out the costs of the work done. The dismantling, the removing of debris, the tile work, the ceiling work, the electricity points and wiring, the plumbing ...everything is measured and worked out properly. it shows for certain that the payment made was almost double to the amount of work done till now by Monika.

BUT THE QUOTATION SAID A DIFFERENT STORY. IT SHOWED THAT PURVI HAD MADE A PAYMENT OF RS. 3,75,000...AND THE WORK DONE WAS FOR RS. 7,50,000.

This was a DISPUTE in itself. Neither of the two parties were going to admit that the other was right. So Vikram suggests Purvi not to make any more payments and talk to Monika and sort out the matter. If need be, she should talk to that friend who had suggested Monika's name.

Purvi calls Prakash and discusses the matter, but no conclusion is reached.

A week later, Purvi calls Vikram again and asks him to come home. It is the same matter again. THE RENOVATION. Things have not moved an inch from where Vikram had left them a week ago. Vikram goes to her house and they discuss what options they have. In the meantime, MR Nand kishore comes and joins them and says hello to Vikram. MR Nand Kishore says that he is not happy with Monika's work and behaviour, so he wants to terminate her contract. He asks Vikram to suggest them somebody who can finish the job satisfactorily and as early as possible. Vikram assures him that he will help in getting the work done but firstly they should inform Prakash and Monika, that we are not happy with your work and that your services are no longer required, so we are giving the contract to somebody else. Purvi says Prakash is talking to Monika about this whole goof-up.

Vikram gets a call from home. He attends the call and then says to Purvi and MR Nand Kishore that he has to go as he has some urgent work at home. He says he will come again and then they can discuss the matter. MR Nand kishore offers him a drink and Vikram says maybe some other time. He leaves the room. Purvi comes out with him discussing what was to be done next and Vikram very casually asks her who this guy Prakash is, as he is the one who has recommended the architect and has not been able to sort out the problems. Hearing PRAKASH'S name, Purvi blushes and smiles. She lowers her head and says he is the son of the lady who supplies uniform at the school. Vikram does not like this BLUSHING. She only blushed when he himself used to look at her with love and affection. Right now, she was blushing on hearing Prakash's name. What was the matter with her? This was a very wrong signal; and the way she smiled and her head went down was saying a story in itself.

YOU DO NOT BLUSH FOR THE SON OF SOMEONE YOU KNOW REMOTELY AND THAT TOO, PROFESSIONALLY. YOU DO NOT BLUSH FOR SOMEONE WHO IS JUST A FRIEND. YOU

BLUSH WHEN SOMETHING IS GOING ON BETWEEN YOU AND HIM AND THE THIRD PERSON ASKS YOU ABOUT HIM. AND VIKRAM IS THAT THIRD PERSON RIGHT NOW.

Vikram goes out of the gate, sits in his car, fakes a smile, waves to Purvi, and drives off. His mind is in an overdrive thinking about Purvi and seeking answers to that one question. WHY DID SHE BLUSH? He knows something is going on. This woman he loves so badly and who in turn says that she loves him more than he loves her, is two-timing him. A few things from the recent past were already disturbing him. She had blocked him for three hours just a few days back saying she had gone to the DOCTOR and did not want him(vikram) to disturb her. Was Prakash the DOCTOR ....? Then there was that argument in which she had clearly said that she wanted a boyfriend and not a husband. Maybe this guy is the new boyfriend and he (Vikram) is the husband who is wanted no more. He smiles. She did keep a few KARWACHAUTH VRATS for him .... and then there was that pleasure-giving machine dialogue. When a woman tells a man, that she is not a pleasure-giving machine, it is a signal. It is a signal that she is not enjoying his company anymore. That she is giving more than she is getting. But, when you are in love, it is not about giving or taking; it is about SHARING.

DEEP INSIDE, VIKRAM KNOWS THAT THINGS ARE OVER BETWEEN HIM AND PURVI. LOVE HAS EVAPORATED AND FORMED DARK CLOUDS OF SEX; AND THOSE CLOUDS ARE NOT GOING TO RAIN LOVE. THEY ARE GOING TO RAIN LUST. AND LUST IS WHAT PURVI WANTS.

Vikram is about to enter his colony when Purvi calls. She asks if he has reached home. He says he hasn't yet. Then, as he wants to asks her if Prakash is mature and responsible enough (age wise) to handle this money and work dispute she is having with Monika, one word - a wrong word in a right sentence - rushes out of Vikram's mouth, as if waiting for this moment, a moment of glory, a moment of getting inked in Vikram's story. He says it and wonders how could he. But he has no regrets. For this is his own word, and he owns it. This is a word that changes the entire script of Vikram's love story and he watches things unfold, helplessly. He asks her: *Uss CHUTIYE ki umar kya hai* (What is the age of that asshole)? and pat comes the reply: How DARE you use this word?!

Vikram uses this CHU word as if it is some sort of a cult in Hindi dictionary. He uses it very often and uses it for everybody. Even for himself. It never hurt anyone and never mattered to anyone. But it hurt Purvi and it mattered to her. It was used for a man she BLUSHED for. It was used for a man who, according to her, was a FRIEND. It was a word used by a man she had loved and wanted to marry .... And used for a man only she knew what he was to her.

Vikram is not going to take his word back, he has said what he has said. He is not going to backout or apologize. Purvi says I DON'T WANT TO TALK TO YOU. KEEP THE PHONE DOWN. Vikram says DON'T CALL ME EVER AGAIN; and she disconnects.

LOVE IS SUPPOSED TO BE COLOURFUL, BUT HERE, IT HAS SHADES OF GREY ......

Na tha maloom mohabbat mein, chot khayenge ik din ....

Tujhse dil lagake gaafil, pachhtayenge ik din ....

Jaan dete hain tujhpe, maloom tha lekin ....

Na tha maloom, ki jaan se jayenge ik din ....

THE LULL BEFORE THE STORM

Vikram is looking blankly at his laptop, trying hard to concentrate on a few particular stocks. The market is as dull and as flat as his life right now. There is no excitement and no ups and downs in these stocks. He doesn't feel like working on them as much as he doesn't feel like working on his relationship with Purvi. He has a feeling of resentment. How could she treat him like trash? He has been crazy for her all these years, loving her and ignoring everything else, as if nothing else mattered. Yet, here she is, objecting to a word, used for a man he doesn't even know and she is making an issue out of it (doesn't even want to talk). Is that word worth giving up your relationship? Or is that MAN worth giving up your love story? OR IS IT BOTH? It is out of Vikram's understanding ....

Vikram should understand that anybody can be Purvi's friend. If an unknown sales person can be given the phone number, an unknown man in the hospital lobby can be given the phone number, then why cannot she share her number or be friends with the uniform supplier's son? At least she knows who he is; and this is not the first time she has acknowledged another man showing interest in her. There have been so many instances of her telling him about different men and women. Vikram should have got used to her playful nature by now. He should have known by now that Purvi is approachable and looks for fun. He should have known that she can be friends with anybody. That he is not her world any more. THOSE WERE DIFFERENT DAYS AND THEY ARE GONE FOR NOW ....

This is the perfect time to step back. He and Purvi have not been talking and his BRAIN has all the reasons in the world to sit with his HEART, face to face, and tell it that there was life when she was not there, and there will be life when she will not be there. So, he should NOT LOSE HEART and BE HAPPY. But the BRAIN also knows that the HEART will not listen to him. It will reason with him. It'll tell him that he is a good man and a kind man. That he should forgive and forget. That he loves her and love is the greatest virtue of all. That he has promised to be by Purvi's side, at all times. GOOD OR BAD.

AND IN THE END .... HEART WINS OVER BRAIN. It forgets that it has been played with, twisted badly, hurt very often and broken on a regular basis. It forgets what it feels like at that very moment. IT BLAMES THE BRAIN FOR MANIPULATING MATTERS AND MAKING THEM WORSE. From there on, it decides to take the matter in its own hands and build up the relation once again, and starts putting all the broken pieces together.

Vikram is sitting in his office and thinking about Purvi. They have not talked for the last four days. A feeling of GUILT is setting in. He is never at fault, but because he is an emotional person, he always tries to blame himself. He always says: your conscience is the MIRROR to your DEEDS. It will never tell you whether you are right or wrong, but it will always tell you what you exactly did. So, he knows what he did and he knows he is not wrong, but because he loves her, he is ready to be wronged. So, he is telling himself: you love her, and love for you is all about giving. You have promised to be by her side at all times. FUCK THIS PRAKASH. Stop doubting her and rather, help her. It is you who is ruining the relationship. Call her this one time and make amends for where things have gone wrong. So, he decides to put their personal differences aside once and for all and help Purvi out.

Vikram knows that Purvi has been having a tough time lately. Her DAD is not well, kids are home and around...not helping but increasing the work load, the house renovation has stopped and Monika has been sort of blackmailing to extract the money from her. There is debris and trash all around the house, the kitchen is in a bad shape, the two bedrooms are full of dust, and there is nobody to help or share the burden. Also, he has promised MR Nand Kishore that he will sort out this Monika matter .... So, he will.

Vikram calls an acquaintance who is into interior designing and asks him if he is ready to take an unfinished job, left midway by some other designer. He provides him with all the details and gives a personal guarantee that he will not face any financial problems with the concerned client. After assuring him and after getting the assurance that he will complete the project, he calls Purvi. Purvi does not pick the call. After waiting for some time, he messages her: Good afternoon. How is the work going? I have spoken to a friend who is willing to take your project and complete it. Let me know if I can be of any help?

Vikram has checked his phone a minimum twenty times and Purvi has yet not replied. THE HEART IS STARTING TO SINK AND THE BRAIN IS GETTING STRONGER AGAIN. It is once again trying to dominate the heart. The heart is saying that she might be busy with daddy or the kids or in the kitchen, and the brain is suggesting that she is with PRAKASH. The RIGHT-WRONG conflict has started to shake him up. THE HEART IS TRYING TO DEFEND PURVI AND THE BRAIN IS VERY STRONGLY BLAMING HER.

PURVI REPLIES TO VIKRAM'S WATSAPP AFTER THREE HOURS. ALL THIS WHILE SHE HAS BEEN BUSY WITH

PRAKASH AT HER HOUSE, TAKING THE MEASUREMENTS OF THE CEILINGS AND THE WALLS AND GOD KNOWS WHAT ELSE....

At 6:15 pm in the evening, Vikram receives Purvi's message saying: Good evening. Will let you know if needed. Thanks. Vikram asks about the work and she says it is on standstill. He asks why and she says I don't know. He asks if she had spoken to M0nika or Prakash and she sends him a PDF file containing all the details of the work done and the money quoted by Monika. Vikram has a look at it and knows this is some serious stuff. He knows PURVI ALONE WILL NOT BE ABLE TO SORT IT OUT. He messages her that she will not be able to sort out this money issue. She asks why and, in the meantime, he writes it will be a difficult task. She replies if this is the answer, then thank you. The normal conversation which was supposed to be a patch up conversation is turning bad yet again. She is talking in a formal manner and to the point, and Vikram is not liking it. He tries to soften himself and writes that he is coming back as always (as is the condition put by her, that she will do all the wrongs and he will have to say sorry every time. This is her way of telling him that he has to woo her all the time) as he is the one who has to be sorry. To this she replies that he had used inappropriate words for someone which she did not like ....and he should be sorry for the same.

NOW THIS WAS GETTING NASTY. Vikram did not like her starting the same thing all over again. He asks her why would she stop talking to him for somebody else? She says she did not and it was him. He says it was her who said I don't want to talk to you, keep the phone. She says she had said that a thousand times before and will say it again. It is he who has to decide whether he wants to accept her like that or not. He says every time they argued, he said sorry because the argument was about them. But this time she wanted him to say sorry for somebody else. She says she does not want to discuss further on this baseless topic. The conversation was not going in the right direction, so he decides that he will go and meet her and sort it once and for all. He decides that he will go .... hug her, kiss her, and will resolve things as always. But he did not know that there will be no hugs and no kisses this time .... THE TIME HAD COME FOR THE CURTAINS.

THE TSUNAMI

At around 8:30 pm, Vikram messages Purvi that he will be coming to her place after dinner. She does not reply. He messages her again at 9:30 pm that he will be reaching in ten minutes. Again, she does not reply. He reaches her house, parks the car across the road and messages her that he has reached. Still, she does not reply. He waits for five minutes and then walks towards the house, opens the gate and crosses the driveway. He sees Ananya in the kitchen and waves to her. From inside, she says mom is feeding nanu (grandfather) and will take some time. He says it is okay and starts strolling in the driveway. After about fifteen minutes he goes to his car, takes the cigarette pack from the side console and lights a cigarette. He takes a few drags and throws the cigarette away. Then he again walks towards the house.

He goes towards the kitchen and Purvi opens the door for him. The welcome smile which is always there whenever she sees him is missing today and there is this grave look on her face. There is no exchange of pleasantries and she straight-away asks him to follow her to the bedroom. Vikram is feeling some tension in the air and sees that Purvi is not looking comfortable. But since he has come to meet her and sort out the issues, he starts the conversation and says that he has spoken to a friend who is ready to take the project. But before giving the project to a third person, they should first settle their disputes with Monika and take it on paper that she will not be troubling them. For, after losing a contract midway, these people go to labour courts or file a civil suit, which will further cause more delay and more trouble. So, she should talk to Prakash and Monika and sort things out.

The moment Vikram takes Prakash's name, Purvi blushes and smiles. He is numbed. This was the second time this week that she had blushed and smiled in a very mysterious manner, just on the mention of this mysterious man. Vikram asks her why she is smiling, to which she doesn't answer but smiles and blushes again. Vikram loses his cool. He is irritated by her coldness to his question. He asks her who this Prakash is to her and why is she smiling and blushing? Still, she does not answer. Vikram is looking at her blankly and is feeling like an idiot who is being kept in the dark. Her silence is killing him, and her smile is giving him a thousand silent answers. It is clearly indicating that she is hiding something from him and does not wish to open her mouth and make herself a culprit of some wrongdoing.

In the meantime, Chhotu comes in the room and sees that Vikram uncle is looking tense and his mother is standing like a statue, not answering his questions. He asks them to sit and clear whatever the misunderstandings are. Purvi never wanted her kids to be involved in her personal matters. Her relation with Vikram was too personal and nobody except them both (Vikram and Purvi) knew about the intimacy they shared with each other. The kids did know about their college-time romance and that they wished to get married but could not. They knew that their mother was very close to Vikram uncle, but they did not know the level of this closeness. And now, this man, who she is supposed to be close to, is asking her questions. He is pointing fingers at her, her character. At this point, Purvi erupts like a volcano which has just become active ....

FOR THE FIRST TIME IN THESE YEARS, VIKRAM GETS TO SEE HER REAL AVATAR (PERSONA). He has just pushed her to the limits and she is ready to pounce on him. On top of her voice, as if to make everybody in the house and the neighbours above and on two sides hear, she yells on his face: Can't I have my own life? Can't I have friends? Who is this man to tell me what to do and what not to do? Vikram is clean-bowled by this yorker. He was not expecting Purvi to shout at him. Chhotu, who had gone to the kitchen after telling them to sort out things peacefully, and Ananya, who was in the next room with nanu, come rushing. Purvi, on seeing both her children entering the room, repeats what she had just said in their absence. Who is this man to interfere in my life? Can't I have friends? Can't I live life the way I want to? She repeats these three sentences minimum thrice and on top of her voice. All this while Vikram has been requesting her to calm down and speak softly. THE WOMAN WHO HAD FULL CONTROL OVER VIKRAM AND HIS LIFE WAS NOW CREATING AN IMPRESSION THAT VIKRAM WAS TRYING TO CONTROL HER AND THE GAAFIL STILL COULD NOT GET IT. HE IS SO MUCH IN LOVE.

The kids ask their mother to calm down. Ananya asks what the fuss was all about. Vikram says he wants clarity in his relationship with Purvi. He says if she wants to end her relationship with him (Vikram), it should be in an amicable manner, with no hard feelings. The kids again ask them to sort it out among themselves and leave the room. Once they leave the room, she again starts saying the same thing, without making any eye contact with him, looking blankly at the wall above him. Vikram is constantly looking at her, trying to make eye contact. At one point he says to her: Are you cross-eyed? She briefly smiles on hearing what Vikram has just said to her and sits on the side of the bed. She had been standing all this while. Vikram goes and sits by her side. As always, he tries to put his arm around her but she pushes him back. Never in seven years, had she behaved like this. Whenever he was angry with her, or she was angry with him, they used to hug and make up. But this time, she was behaving like she had never loved him; like she wanted him no more in her life; like the loyalties had already shifted towards somebody else.

Vikram knows that Purvi has mood swings. He also knows that she has fits of severe anxiety. This he knows from college days. That is why he has been maintaining his cool and trying to calm her down. But how long could he control his emotions? He could see her drifting away from him. He could see the sudden change in her. What he could not see was that she had changed a long time back. He could not see that nothing except change was permanent in this world, and she wanted change. He could not see that his love was not fulfilling, it was incomplete. He, for one, very firmly believed in his love, and thought that it was love that the whole world believed in. But it was not so. The world does not believe in philosophies or sweet talks or emotions. It believes in practicalities; it believes in action and in physicality. It does not believe in giving more. It believes in getting more.

And for Purvi, it was just a matter of time before she revolted and went against Vikram and his love. AND THIS WAS THE TIME. THIS WAS THE MOMENT DESTINY HAD CHOSEN FOR HER TO KICK VIKRAM OUT OF HER LIFE. She pushes him hard. The message is conveyed. It is clear that she wants no patch-up this time. This is the time when our MR COOL loses his cool. He is so taken aback by her unexpected behaviour, that he does something in a fit of rage, something that he would never have done in his senses. He says that falling in love with her was his biggest mistake. He says he is dead for her and storms out of the room angrily, not realising that her kids had heard whatever he had said. Nothing matters to him right now. He is a broken man with a broken heart. He knows things are over. He just wants to be out of this place. That's it.

Vikram is blank and driving towards home. He is not able to focus on anything. He lights up a cigarette and tries to remember what had just happened at Purvi's house but to no help. The trauma he has just gone through has been deleted from the memory card of his brain. This is how his body and brain react in times of extreme crisis. It switches off the entire system and he becomes a body without emotions. A body that will not react in any which way. So, he is just driving and he reaches the point from where he had taken a U-turn when Purvi had torn apart his shirt and had begged him to come back to her a few years ago. The incident comes to his mind in a flash and he decides to take a U-turn and go back to her one last time, just to try and put some life in his already dead relationship with Purvi.

The only thing which did not flash in his mind was ...last time it was Purvi who begged him to come back. And this time it was him who was begging her not to go. The last time it was him who wanted to walk out on her but did not because he loved her. And this time, it is her who wants to walk out on him because now she loves somebody else.

Vikram takes a U-turn, drives to Purvi's house, parks the car at the same place across the road and walks towards the house. There is nobody in the kitchen and it is locked from inside. He messages Purvi that he is standing outside the kitchen. After a while, Chhotu comes and opens the door. Vikram smiles at him and goes towards the bedroom. Purvi is sitting on the bed and the moment Vikram enters the room, she asks him why he is back. Vikram does not reply and sits on the sofa, silently. She asks him if he has to say something. If yes, he must say it soon, as the kids were supposed to be back in the room. This was an indicator that you must leave now. But our careless man does not understand the signal. He is too simple a man. A GAAFIL. He is sitting silently, blankly, not saying anything. As if the GODS were themselves going to intervene and make things all goody-goody. But it is not going to happen. How can the Gods go back on what they have written themselves in his destiny?

It is supposed to get worse from here. And it will. And it does. Purvi asks him why has he come back? What is the motive behind his coming back when he had already said that he was dead for her just before leaving, some ten minutes back? Vikram is rattled by her behaviour. She is not talking straight and is taking everything negatively. He is here to give it another try, maybe the last try. To mend things. But she is in no mood of relenting. It seems she has already made up her mind, not to give themselves another chance. Not to give him another chance. That chance has been given to somebody else.

Vikram tries to say that he does not want things to end. And if at all she is hell bent on ending them, he does not want them to end on a sour note. To try to make things normal between them, and be close and talk, he gets up from the sofa and sits beside her. Just as he comes and sits with her, she shifts further away from him, making him uncomfortable in his own skin. He tries to hug her just like he had tried to hug her fifteen minutes back, and she pushes him back just like she had pushed him fifteen minutes back. It is exactly a repeat of what had happened in this room just fifteen minutes back. Vikram is still very calm and hopeful that she will relent. In this hope, he gets up and tries to hold her, and she struggles to break free. She pushes him back hard and with full force. She is a tall and strong woman who stands 5"6 and weighs 80 kg. He looks her in the eye, and knows that things will never be the same again between them. He pushes her and goes out of the room, not knowing that he has hurt Purvi by mistake. He pushes her and she falls on the bed, her head banging on the wooden side. He goes to his car, lights a cigarette and drives away, knowing that he will never be coming back here again.

Jab manzoor nahin use, milna tumhara ...

Bekaar koshish GAAFIL, kyun ki dobara ...

Jo hoti mohabbat, to jaane naa deti ....

Itna sa bhi tum, na samjhe ishara ......

Vikram is so pained by this turn of events in his life, that he just wants to end it. He does not want to live anymore. The myth (love) he always believed in, is shattered. He himself is shattered. He takes a drag and is contemplating his next move (how to die), when his conscience intervenes and speaks to him. It says to him: IT IS BETTER TO LOSE A WOMAN WHO DOESN'T LOVE YOU, THAN TO DIE FOR A WOMAN YOU LOVE. LIVE FOR PEOPLE WHO LOVE YOU. THERE IS AN ENTIRE WORLD THAT LOVES YOU ...... Vikram goes home.

THE CONSEQUENCE

Vikram is a learned man. He has many philosophies on life and its journey. He knows that: LIFE IS A CONSEQUENCE OF YOUR ACTIONS, AND THE ACTIONS OF THE UNIVERSE. He is going home not knowing that after his action, the universe is going to REACT. There has to be a reaction for every action. That is the law of the universe. He reaches home, parks his car and goes inside. The moment Vikram enters his house, Ayaan and Aryan call him to their bedroom and ask him what he had done. Ayaan asks him to come with him to Purvi's house that very moment. He is surprised to see that the kids are still awake and shocked on why Ayaan is asking him to go with him to Purvi's house. He was not expecting that his kids would be knowing what had happened at Purvi's house. He asks Ayaan what is the matter but instead of answering, he asks him to come with him and says that they will talk on the way.

On the other side, after Vikram left, Ananya goes to the room and sees her mother sobbing. There is a small bruise on her forehead. She knows they had been arguing and takes the bruise as a beating by Vikram. She calls Ayaan and threatens him with dire consequences. Purvi does not clarify things to Ananya as this was the perfect getaway for her. SHE WANTS TO GET RID OF VIKRAM.

Vikram and the kids leave the house silently, not wanting to disturb Anjali by waking her up. Vikram is driving and Ayaan updates him that just two minutes back, Ananya had called and told him that your father has beaten my mother. She was threatening to call the police and said that she will come to our house if we did not bring you with us to their house. Vikram frowns and says he did not beat anybody. Ayaan asks Vikram if he had done anything wrong and he says he has not. In between Ananya calls Ayaan twice on his phone and asks about their whereabouts. Each time, Ayaan says that they are on their way and will reach in another two minutes.

Ananya has always been good at theatrics. Even when she used to fight and argue with her mother, she used to over-react. She used to howl and make a big hue & cry of everything. She used to create such a spectacle of emotions, that a third person view would be as if she was absolutely right and the mother was forcefully proving her wrong. Vikram and family are about to reach Purvi's house when Ananya calls Ayaan again. She is screaming at the top of her voice, saying: You guys haven't reached as yet. I am calling the police. The clock is ticking … tik tock, tik tock, tik tock. Now this was her way of conveying the message to Vikram that the tables had turned; that it was her turn to take revenge on him; it was her turn to do his character bashing. It was him, who had pointed fingers at her character the last time, and now, she has the perfect set-up to give him the same treatment. The girl who has had multiple flings with a number of guys is not ready to tolerate a man who is having an affair with her separated mother. It doesn't matter to her that they have known each other for thirty-two years. The girl who was always at loggerheads with her mom, is now ready to prove to her that she is her saviour.

They reach Purvi's house and Vikram parks the car in front of the house. He is as cold as ice, as calm as a monk, and totally at peace with himself. There is no fear, no anxiety, no emotion at all on his face. He is ready to face the wrath of this unfaithful, uncaring, unloving family. They get down from the car and walk towards the gate. Purvi and her two kids come rushing out of the kitchen towards them. Chhotu advances angrily towards Vikram and tries to slap him in the face, which Vikram somehow manages to dodge. Chhotu grabs Vikram by the neck and tries to squeeze it. Aryan intervenes and holds Chhotu by the arm but before he can raise his hand on Chhotu, Vikram warns Aryan not to do so. In the meantime, Ananya starts hitting Vikram with a stick she had carried with her. Both Ananya and Chhotu are constantly abusing and hitting Vikram. Purvi is standing at a side and watching them abuse him and beat him. Ayaan is repeatedly apologizing to Purvi on his father's behalf, asking her to forgive him and stop this fight, to which Purvi is paying no attention.

Vikram alone is capable of taking care of Purvi and her family (which he considered his own) but he does not want to lose his cool, or be violent with them. He is taking all the beating because this was a family he had loved and these were the children he had treated like his own. He knew they were badly brought up, ill-mannered and could react in any strange manner. A girl who can call her mother a bitch in the middle of the road, and a boy who can shout on his mother for a thing as small as a chapati, can be as rude and as vulgar to him as they can possibly be. He is ready for this humiliation. He knows if he raises his hand, he will not be able to stop himself and Ayaan and Aryan. His kids are helplessly watching their father taking all the beating.

After some time, Ayaan and Aryan somehow manage to get their father out of this mayhem, and they take him away from Purvi and her two kids. They ask him if he is fine and he replies he is all good. Then Vikram asks Aryan if he had raised his hand on Chhotu, to which Aryan replies that Chhotu would have been buried by now if he (Vikram) had not stopped him (Aryan). Purvi is listening this father-son conversation and deep inside she knows very well that if Vikram had wanted, he would have easily beaten up Chhotu. Of course, he will not raise his hand on Ananya, as he is a thorough gentleman and a principled man and will never disrespect a woman. Out of guilt, she asks Ayaan to come with her inside the house, for she wants to explain things to him, and maybe sort out the matter; but Ayaan refuses to go with her. Ananya and Chhotu also oppose this gesture by their mother. They don't want this opportunity of insulting and harassing Vikram, to slip out of their hands. They don't want any compromises.

IN THE MEANWHILE, ANANYA HAS CALLED THE POLICE. In a matter of few minutes, two police vans arrive. Five policemen emerge from the two vans. One of them, Sub Inspector Kanhayya Lal, asks Purvi what the matter is. Ananya says that Vikram had beaten their mother and should be charged for violence and harassment. Chhotu, who is studying law and is a first-year student, behaves as if he is some top-notch advocate. He repeatedly keeps telling Vikram: Just you see... you will now go to jail. The boy who used to call him uncle and used to ask him for every other favour, is now addressing him derogatorily and treating him like a criminal. Purvi is in two minds. She surely wants to get rid of Vikram, but doesn't want to initiate police action against him. Maybe because she loved him once, or maybe because she knows he still loves her and is not wrong.

Ayaan has been strongly defending his father all this while, telling the policemen that they were all family and there was just a misunderstanding and nothing serious had happened. He even tries to persuade Purvi for a compromise and asks her that how could she do this to Vikram when he had loved her more than he had loved his wife. Purvi relents and asks the policemen to go, now that the matter is between families and is sorted. At this point, Ananya feels like she has lost an already-won battle. She cannot let go of this man; the man she wants to see behind bars. She holds her mother by the arm and takes her aside. She says to Purvi that now if she does not file a complaint against Vikram, she, along with Chhotu will go to their father (Ramit) and will never return. She emotionally blackmails her mother and forces her to file a complaint against Vikram. This girl has always been a over-reactor and a master-manipulator and knows very well how to break people and their relationships. It is already 1 am in the night and the drama outside Purvi's house is not over yet.

MR NAND KISHORE COMES OUT OF THE HOUSE TO SEE WHAT WAS HAPPENING. THE POOR FELLOW IS NOT AWARE THAT HIS DAUGHTER AND HER KIDS HAVE JUST HAD A FIGHT WITH THE MAN THEY DEPENDED ON TO SORT OUT THEIR DISPUTES.

Vikram turns around, as he doesn't want MR Nand kishore to see him. He doesn't want to give this old man the trouble of going through the pains of knowing the reality about him and his own daughter. The old man doesn't know till date, that this Vikram is the same guy who was in college with Purvi and who he had rejected as a possible son-in-law. So, Vikram asks Ayaan to ask Purvi to send her father inside. The old man is not well and in the last few months, Vikram has developed a soft corner for him. Purvi goes to her father, says something to him, and takes him inside.

She comes back and asks Sub Inspector Kanhayya Lal for a blank sheet of paper to write the complaint on. The details of the complaint are dictated by Ananya. The girl is now the new BOSS of the family. She has taken all matters in her own hands and is going to make sure that Vikram disappears from their lives forever. They discuss all the points thoroughly with Chhotu, who is the new lawyer of the family. Once finished with writing, they go through all the details written on the paper again, and after they are satisfied that this is how they want to implicate Vikram, they call Sub Inspector Kanhayya Lal and give him the paper. Kanhayya Lal reads it and asks them to reconsider what they had written in it. They say they are sure about what they have written and this is exactly what they want.

Ayaan is not pleased to see Purvi write a complaint against his father. He very lovingly says to Vikram: Till now, I was very sure of aunty, that she is not going to go against you. That she will not file a police complaint. But it looks as if she has chosen sides now. She is doing what Ananya is asking her to do. Vikram is lost in some heavenly world. He knows that he has done no wrong and nothing will happen to him. He just smiles at Ayaan. Kanhayya Lal comes to Vikram and asks him to sign and write his phone number on the paper the complaint is written on. Vikram signs on it without reading the contents of the complaint. Kanhayya Lal says that the complaint has been received and the proceedings (whatever action they have to take) will start in the morning. He asks both the families to go to their houses and then leaves with his entourage.

Before leaving the spot, Purvi says to Vikram: I'm dead for you from now onwards. Now, this was what Vikram had said to her just two hours back. The woman does not even have something original to say to him. She says that and along with her boss and lawyer, goes inside her house.

Kehte the na chhodenge tera saath ....

Har haal mein thamenge tera haath ....

Jab aaya waqt aazmayish ka ...

Rani ne apne he raja ko di maat ....

They may have gone inside, but the matter is not finished yet. A whole new story is going to take shape now. But Vikram is not worried any more. He knows he has the love and support of his two sons to counter the wickedness of Purvi and company. These are the very kids Purvi wanted Vikram to leave for her. These are the very kids who are standing by his side right now, when she herself has left him because of her two children.

AND LOOK AT THE TURN OF EVENTS ... THE EVENING STARTED BY VIKRAM POINTING A FINGER AT PURVI, AND

NOW ALL FINGERS ARE POINTED AT HIM. THE WOMAN WHO WAS BEING ACCUSED OF TREACHERY IS NOW PLAYING A VICTIM CARD AND ACCUSING VIKRAM OF HARASSING HER.

THE WRECKAGE

It's almost 2 O' clock in the night and Vikram is driving back home. Ayaan and Aryan are still having the heebie-jeebies. They have just witnessed a YASH CHOPRA MOVIE CLIMAX involving them all. This is so surreal. Not in their weirdest of dreams could Ayaan and Aryan imagine that they would ever witness their father's love story, live. THIS WAS A LOVE STORY. A love story gone bad. They know that this fantasy trip is not over yet. They know that they are in for many bumpy rides in the days to come.

Aryan is amused with what he has just experienced. He says that it appears as if his father and Purvi aunty were having a teenage love affair. That they had begun from where they had left some thirty years back. Vikram smiles at this observation of his, thinking this is one smart kid. Vikram asks him how could he surmise that. Aryan says they both had acted so naively, when they could have handled it maturely. They should have sat and talked. Vikram says he tried ... Ayaan interrupts and says leave it. The story is over now. They wanted to get rid of you. That's it. If she had loved you, she would not have made the police complaint. Vikram counters him by saying: Purvi never wanted to. Ananya forced her to. Ayaan says: WHATEVER.

They reach home and very quietly sneak into their bedrooms and try to sleep. Ayaan and Aryan are not sleepy at all. They are discussing how the thriller unfolded. This had been a night of terror, confusion, manipulation, betrayal and belief. Ayaan was terrorised from the moment he received Ananya's call. Aryan and Chhotu were confused souls, not getting a taste of the action taking place. Ananya was the one who manipulated and destroyed her mother's relationship. Who was she taking revenge from? Her mother ... who opposed all her relationships? Or Vikram uncle ... who she despised for being too nice to her. Purvi was a perfect picture of betrayal .... A police complaint against a man she said she loved. Vikram stands by his beliefs ...a belief that she loves him and will not harm him, and a belief that he has done no wrong, so will not be harmed. Ayaan and Aryan could not sleep the whole night, whereas Vikram slept the moment he lied on his bed. This was a careless man. A GAAFIL.

The next day in the afternoon, Vikram is sitting in his office and analysing what went wrong, where, why and when. He has all the answers. He knows that the woman (Purvi) has lost her way and is on a path of self-exploration, self-exploitation and self-destruction. He knows that the path she has chosen has no place for him to be her companion. She has been choosing her admirers for a while now and has recently got a new sidekick. He also knows that because he could not be a sidekick, she kicked him out of her life.

Vikram is having coffee and smoking a cigarette. Coffee and cigarette are a good combination and Vikram loves it. Just then, something strikes him and he picks up his phone and dials a number. He is calling the MENTOR MONISHA. He just wants to confirm that the mentor knows the accomplishments of his adherent. Monisha answers the phone but before she can say anything, Vikram introduces himself saying: hello Monisha, good afternoon. This is Vikram. Purvi's friend. She is startled by his call. She had not expected him to call. But, nevertheless, she replies to him, asking why he has called. Vikram inquires if she knows about what had happened between him and Purvi the previous night and she says she knows it all. Then she quotes RICHARD BACH to say: If you love somebody, set them free. If they come back, they are yours and if they don't, they never were. She says that he should let Purvi go. For Vikram, it is not about letting her go; it is about the confirmation that Purvi wants to go. He gets his verification through Monisha's words.

About the quote by Richard Bach, Vikram had read it a long time ago and never believed in it. One of his many philosophies is, that money and women, if they go from your life, they are not going to come back. So, be wise and maintain them. And here is a woman who is trying to sell him one of the notebook-philosophies. He does not respond to what Monisha has just advised him. Instead, he asks her if what Purvi has done to him is right. She says she will stand by her friend (Purvi). He knew the answer beforehand but he just wanted to test the waters. According to Vikram, Monisha had just cleared her mentorship programme with flying colours. This is what you expect from a mentor, never to abandon your pupil. As for the pupil, she is so dedicated to the prophecies of the master, she surely will surpass the mentor one day. She has just achieved a milestone of dumping the same man TWICE.

Ilzaame bewafai tujh pe bhi hai....

ki bigaada mere pyar ko gaafil ....

Na tha malum ki dogi ek din ....

Chot mere aitbaar ko gaafil....

Next day, in the evening, Vikram receives a call from the corrupt and conspiring Sub Inspector Kanhayya Lal. He wants to meet Vikram in regards to the complaint made by Purvi. Vikram knows this was to come and he is mentally in tune with the circumstances. He knows nobody can do him no harm unless he gives them an opportunity to; and, the opportunity will only be given to maintain the decorum of love. Vikram says he can meet him after office hours. Kanhayya Lal is more than okay with whatever time and place Vikram suggests. He knows the man he is dealing with is innocent and wealthy. Moreover, he is overwhelmed by Vikram's personality, his silence and politeness. He had watched Vikram the previous night. The man had just not responded in any way to Purvi's family's aggressiveness and cross-questioning by the police. Normally people break under police pressure, but this man maintained his composure. They fix a place and time. The time is 8:30 pm and the place is a market at a midpoint.

Vikram reaches the designated place. It is a small market with a few shops. The Sub Inspector is already there waiting for him. Vikram lights a cigarette and asks him why he wanted to meet. He says that Purvi had come to the police station in the morning and wanted to file a fresh complaint. He says that he told her that she had already given a complaint to him and that two different complaints cannot be given by a person for the same incident. Vikram is listening. Kanhayya Lal further says that Purvi wanted to level some serious charges like that of violence and harassment against him (Vikram), but he dissuaded her. He adds that he has spoken to the SHO, and the SHO is asking for Rs. Ten thousand for his help in not taking a second complaint. He says that he himself will be taking another Rs. Ten thousand for helping him and not harassing him. Vikram smiles. He knows what Kanhayya Lal is saying is absolutely correct.

Vikram gives him Rs. Ten thousand then and there. He does not want any more problems for himself. He is already pained by what has happened between him and Purvi, and now he doesn't want the police guys to make a mockery of his love story. He just wants to be out of this mess. Vikram says to Kanhayya Lal that the balance amount he will pay once the matter is sorted i.e., once the complaint is taken back by Purvi. What Vikram doesn't know is that the complaint is not going to be taken back and he will be paying many more Rs. Ten thousands to these guys ....

Just two days later, Kanhayya Lal calls Vikram again and asks for the remaining Rs. Ten thousand. Vikram asks him about the complaint and Kanhayya Lal says that Vikram should not worry about that. He assures him that it is taken care of and no case will be filed against him. Vikram goes to the police station and pays the outstanding balance. He thanks Kanhayya Lal for his help and leaves. On the way back, Vikram is smoking a cigarette and feeling relieved.

The tiger thinks he is out of the circus and can roam the jungle freely, but he doesn't know that they have tamed him and converted the circus into a jungle. He is not going to be free. He is going to remain in the cage.

The next afternoon, Vikram is in office when Kanhayya Lal calls. He had met him just last night and paid up. Kanhayya Lal had assured him that all would be fine. So, why was he calling now? What was he up to? Vikram takes the call and asks if everything is fine. Kanhayya Lal says: Purvi madam is here. She wants an apology. You will have to come. Vikram says that he is in office and a bit busy right now and cannot come. If it is about saying sorry, he can say it over the phone. Please give the phone to madam. Kanhayya Lal says she doesn't want to talk on phone. She wants a written apology. So, he will have to come there. Vikram very politely says that he will not be able to come.

AFTER AN HOUR OR SO, SUMER SINGH CALLS ....

BACK TO THE FUTURE

Vikram and Ayaan are standing in a corner and Sumer Singh arrives. The drill is over. He goes to the room that Purvi and Ananya are sitting in. They talk for another half an hour. After that, Sumer Singh comes to Vikram and says: Madam wants to press the charge of Section 376. Come along, I will listen to your story too. He asks Vikram to follow him to the room. Vikram and Ayaan enter the room and stand on one side. Purvi and Ananya are sitting on chairs and the emotional makeup on their faces is saying all that Vikram wants to hear. It is saying out loud that YOU ARE GONE, MISTER! You are finished.

Sumer Singh asks Purvi and Ananya to leave the room. They want to sit and witness the shocks Sumer Singh is going to give to Vikram, but Sumer Singh doesn't want to give them this pleasure. He knows that he has to play even with both the parties if he was to extort money from them (0bviously Vikram). So, he asks Purvi and Ananya to leave the room. They go out. Then he asks Ayaan also to leave the room. But Ayaan is firm about not leaving. Sumer Singh very politely asks him again to go out of the room. But the young man does not move an inch. He looks at Vikram. Vikram looks at Ayaan in the eye as if assuring him that all will be fine and that he should not worry. Ayaan knows his father too well. He knows that nobody can take him for a ride unless and until he himself wants to be taken for a ride. He goes and waits outside. Vikram is asked to take a chair right in front of Sumer Singh. One of the constables closes the room from inside.

Inside, there are five policemen surrounding Vikram. Sumer Singh is sitting across the table, one is on his left, one is on Vikram's right, and two are towering over Vikram, ready to pounce on him the moment they get an indication from Sumer Singh. The scene is stolen from a Bollywood crime thriller where the accused is intimidated and pressurised to admit that he has committed a crime. But Vikram is no criminal and he has committed no crime.

THE INTERROGATION BEGINS.

Sumer Singh: Look mister, a case is going to be filed against you and you will go to jail. Answer only to what is asked of you.

Vikram is a polished guy. Always polite, always respecting others, and expecting others to be the same with him. Now here, this Sub Inspector Sumer Singh, almost sixteen years younger to him, just out of police training college and having his first posting at a police station, is talking rudely with him. He doesn't like it. He replies ....

Vikram: Sir, I'm talking respectfully with you. You also please talk respectfully.

Sumer Singh and company were not expecting this kind of in-your-face reply from Vikram. Normally, people don't talk like that with policemen, and that too in the police station. They are all blank faced. The surprised expression telling their state of mind. The intimidating are now the intimidated. They know this man has guts. This firm statement by Vikram changes their behaviour towards him. Sumer Singh picks a notepad from the table, reads it and asks Vikram...

Sumer Singh: You know Purvi from 1988, you were in the same college.

Vikram: Yes.

Sumer Singh: You stopped meeting in 1990.

Vikram: Yes.

Sumer Singh: You both met again in 2013.

Vikram: Yes.

Sumer Singh: You had physical relations in college times.

Now this is something new for Vikram. something out of the blue. He cannot understand who is the plotter? HE OR SHE? Whose script was this? HIS OR HERS? This is so inane, so insane. He is wondering, how can he question him like that and how can Purvi share her almost incorrect personal details with a man she doesn't know. It doesn't matter if he is a policeman. It doesn't matter if she wants to implicate him (Vikram) in a false case. Those were college days and they were adolescents. They were in love and wanted to get married; and here, he or she is saying they had physical relations! This is absolute rubbish, ridiculously false. Instead of answering, he counterquestions Sumer Singh ...

Vikram: Is Purvi saying this?

Sumer Singh: Yes, she is saying you had physical relations.

Chahat per apni, guroor tha gaafil ...

guroor per apne, maghroor tha gaafil ....

Tootega guroor, aur honge pashemaan ....

Kyun kar tu itna, majboor tha gaafil ....

Vikram knows that this is not Purvi's doing. Either it is Sumer Singh, or it is Ananya. they are fabricating a story. But because she is collaborating with either of them, that makes her equal participant in the wrongdoing. The second thing is, if, and it is an if, if indeed he and Purvi had physical relations, as was being claimed, the relations were totally consensual. They were not forced. And anything that is not forced or on pretext of any false promises, cannot be termed as rape. And if, again it is if, if he had raped her in college, then why did she not complain then? Add to that, why did she get into a relationship with him again, that too after 25 years? BUT WHO IS GOING TO PUT THESE QUESTIONS TO SUMER SINGH AND COMPANY? AND WHO IS GOING TO ANSWER THEM? THIS IS THEIR DOMAIN AND THE QUESTIONS ARE ALL SUPPOSED TO BE THEIRS.

Vikram: There was nothing like physical relations. We loved each other and wanted to get married.

Then Vikram shows Sumer Singh some recent messages and videos sent to him by Purvi on WhatsApp. Sumer Singh sees them and is google-eyed. This is one hell of a shocker for Sumer Singh. Now he knows this man is not guilty. He knows he will have to let him go. But how can he let a fish slip out of his net? He asks Vikram if he had stored or saved this chat. Vikram replies in a yes. Then he asks Vikram why he did not delete those messages or videos? Vikram says he never does and never cared. He says there must be tens of thousands of messages from different people in his WhatsApp. THE GAAFIL NEVER KNEW THAT HIS CARELESSNESS WILL ONE DAY SAVE HIS LIFE.

THE BOUNTY

Sumer Singh wants to roast his fish and eat it too. So, he says to Vikram that he wants to talk to him alone. Vikram says he is fine with it. They go out of the room. Ayaan is just outside, waiting for his father to come out. He is relieved to see him come out. Vikram holds his hand and asks him to come with him. Sumer Singh tries to object but Vikram says it is okay if he comes. Purvi and Ananya curiously watch them go with Sumer Singh. They are still under the impression that they have nailed Vikram. But they do not know that Vikram's belief in God is going to save him and save him how!!!

The all-cunning Sumer Singh takes them to another empty room and says to Vikram that he is ready to help but his help is chargeable. He says he knows that Vikram is innocent. He says sometimes even the courts know that a woman is taking advantage of women-friendly laws and framing a man, but they are helpless. But in his case, there is no need of registering a case as he has himself seen the evidence. So, he will not frame him wrongly and will rather help him out. But he wants to know how Vikram is going to return the favour? Vikram looks him in the eye and says, ask what you want. It will be taken care of.

Sumer Singh is nervous and wants to play safe. Asking for a bribe directly is a crime in itself. So, he is trying to build a story around the money he is going to ask for. He says to Vikram that if he wants to get out of this mess he will have to co-operate (co-operation is an indirect way of asking for money). He says it is all in his hands. He says he can implicate him on Purvi's complaint (falsely, of course) or he can save him by telling her that she is as much a partner in this so-called crime as Vikram is. Vikram agrees to what he is saying. He knows these people can frame anybody to make a quick buck. He is no different. In fact, he knows he will have to pay much more than what a normal person would have paid in these circumstances. His looks and the personality he has, they are screaming that he is an ATM. Sumer Singh just has to insert his credit card and the money will start pouring.

Sumer Singh starts negotiating with Vikram. He asks Vikram how much money he could pay for getting himself out of this rut. Vikram says it is him who has to tell how much he wants. Sumer Singh says that Vikram must have spent lakhs on Purvi in all these years, taking her out on fancy dinners, giving her fancy gifts, and maybe helping her financially too. Vikram does not respond to this comment of his. He did spend lakhs, but that was none of Sumer Singh's business. And why should he acknowledge Sumer Singh's claims. That will give him more fire power. So, he keeps mum on this.

Sumer Singh is running out of patience and finally asks Vikram to pay up Rs. Two lakh fifty thousand, give and take, and then he will be a free man. Ayaan, who has been listening this conversation silently, immediately says that they will PAY. He wants to free his father from Purvi and Sumer Singh's claws. Sumer Singh smiles and says: You get the money and I will go and talk to Purvi. He leaves them there and goes where Purvi and Ananya are waiting for him in anticipation that Vikram is going to be arrested and sent to jail. Not knowing, that their arrangement with Sumer Singh had failed. That their plotting had failed. That truth had finally prevailed (the money being paid was not a bribe but a ritual).

In the meantime, Ayaan rushes to a nearby ICICI BANK ATM and withdraws Rs. Two lakh fifty thousand from his bank account using all four of his credit and debit cards. He is back in the police station in ten minutes.

Sumer Singh, in very plain and simple words, explains to Purvi and her daughter that he has seen the videos and read the messages on WhatsApp. He says it all indicates that whatever it was between Vikram and you, was consensual and not forced. He says no action can be taken if you have been party to the misadventures. He says the only thing he can do to help them is that he can request Vikram to not disturb you in future if you don't want any relations with him. He says he is going to call Vikram in the room and will initiate compromise proceedings. There is nothing more he can do for them. He asks a constable to call Vikram and Ayaan.

Vikram comes and sits in front of Sumer Singh. Purvi and Ananya are now standing on a side. This is what love, truth, time, and fate do to you. In the afternoon, Purvi and Ananya were sitting as accusers and Vikram and Ayaan were standing as the guilty ones. By the night, Vikram and Ayaan are sitting as free birds and Purvi and Ananya are standing as defeated souls. There is a daughter in the room, who wanted to destroy Vikram. And there is a son in the room, who has given him a life line, who himself is his life line.

Sumer Singh asks Purvi to write a compromise note and sign it. Vikram says that he no longer wants to be a part of Purvi's father's will, so his name should be duly removed from the will. He wants this to be mentioned clearly in the compromise note. Purvi writes it all, knowing well that she has not only lost her case, but also the man she once loved. Purvi is upset that her victim card has failed, but to save herself the embarrassment of accepting that she herself was wrong and Vikram was right, she says to Vikram, THE TRUST IS GONE. Now, this was strange, if not hilarious. The entire love story went kaput just because of the trust factor. The woman who could not define her relationship with Prakash, was telling Vikram that she had lost trust in him. It was as if, his conviction would have maintained her trust in him.

Sumer Singh asks Ananya if she wants to say something to Vikram, and the girl is stupefied. She is upset that her plans have failed. She had planned to demean him, use all kinds of derogatory words for him. She wanted to prove and treat Vikram like a criminal. But it was not to be. The man who had treated her like his own daughter, does not deserve to be treated badly. THE GODS WERE ON HIS SIDE TONIGHT.

Purvi signs the compromise note and gives it to Sumer Singh. He then asks Vikram to sign it. After Vikram has signed, Sumer Singh asks Ananya to click a picture of the note and save it in her mobile. She does as asked. Then Sumer Singh asks the mother-daughter duo if there is anything else he can do for them. They are speechless. They say thank you and leave with heavy hearts. But instead of going home, they go and stand outside the police station. Purvi wants to talk to Ayaan.

Sumer Singh asks Vikram if they have arranged the money. Ayaan says the money is in the car. Then he asks him for a copy of the compromise note and very firmly says that he wants a hardcopy duly signed by him. He does not want to leave any loose ends, for he doesn't trust this Sumer Singh and Purvi aunty. Kanhayya Lal had already extorted Rs. Twenty thousand and the matter was just as it was; in fact, it got worse. From a complaint of pushing, it transformed into a complaint of harassment. And from a complaint of harassment, it transformed into a complaint of RAPE. So, he does not want to take any chances. They will have a duly signed copy of the compromise note, and if tomorrow anybody tries to be smart, then he or she should be ready to face their ire this time around. ENOUGH OF BEING NICE TO THIS CROOKED WORLD.

Ayaan goes to get the money. He sees Purvi and Ananya standing in front of the gate. He hears Purvi asking Ananya to talk to

Ayaan, but Ananya doesn't move. Perhaps, because of the guilt. Ayaan is also in no mood of having a goody-goody conversation with them. He respected Purvi aunty as his father's best friend. He knows all about their teenage love story. He knows that they were in love and wanted to get married. He knows his father was dumped because he was not rich enough then. He knows that his father had his sympathies for Purvi aunty. And he is now witness to what his father has got in return for his sympathies. Another heartbreak. Last time, it was the father (MR NAND KISHORE), and he was forgiven and forgotten. This time, it is the daughter (PURVI), and eventually she will be forgiven but not forgotten. Ayaan knows his father does not believe in grudges; he very firmly believes in forgiveness.

Sumer Singh goes to his office and gets a photocopy of the compromise note. He comes back and gives it to Vikram. It has his signature with date and his phone number written on it. Now it is time to pay back. Sumer Singh does not want to take the money in the police station. He also does not want to take the money himself. So, he asks Vikram to pay the money to Kanhayya Lal. Vikram knows how this machinery works. He knows Sumer Singh is afraid of taking the money himself, fearing he might be framed for accepting the bribe. Vikram has no apprehensions in handing over the money to Kanhayya Lal. He calls Kanhayya Lal and asks him to come to the parking area and take the money.

Though Vikram is not clear as to who was trying to frame him, he still thanks Sumer Singh for his help and efforts. In his eyes, all four of them were the culprits. Kanhayya Lal looked like a typical schemer and extractor. Sumer Singh is a fresh recruit and wanted some easy and quick money. Purvi is having a multiple love life and wanted to get rid of him. Ananya felt disrespected and did not like him for his involvement in her affairs and that was a reason enough to extract revenge. The story has so many loose ends that it is really confusing to assume what transpired, or conspired in the last five days. He has no knowledge of what happened at Purvi's house after the pushing episode. He has no idea of what Kanhayya Lal told Sumer Singh about the complaint and him. Maybe he had asked Sumer Singh to extract more money from him. But whatever it was, he was made a scapegoat, and a lot of money was plucked out from him. Yet, Vikram doesn't want to get involved in any kind of blame game. He is happy that it is all over.

Vikram and Ayaan are sitting in the car and Kanhayya Lal comes and says hello to them. Vikram opens the passenger seat door and asks him to get in and sit. Kanhayya Lal gets in and closes the door. Vikram asks Ayaan to hand over the money to him. Ayaan gives Kanhayya Lal the bag containing the money. He opens the bag and his eyes widen just at the sight of the amount of money there is in the bag. He says: Vikram sir, I have never taken more than Rs. Twenty thousand as bribe in my entire service, and this new recruit has taken lakhs from you. Vikram just smiles at him. He continues: Sir, why did you pay so much money? You are not a culprit or a criminal, you should have spent a night in jail and taken bail tomorrow. Vikram smiles again. Either this Kanhayya Lal was an idiot who doesn't know what going to jail means for a family man, or he is jealous of Sumer Singh making so much money. Vikram knows one thing for sure, that his sympathy is fake and he has colluded with Sumer Singh in the extortion.

Kanhayya Lal gets down from the car and Vikram thanks him for his help. Kanhayya Lal goes and gives the bag to Sumer Singh who is standing at the gate of the police station. He keeps the bag on the dashboard of his car and sees Vikram taking a U-turn. Vikram is crossing the police station when he is stopped by Sumer Singh. He asks Vikram to roll down the window of the car. He is all smiles after getting the booty. He gives a few free of cost suggestions to Vikram, that he should be happy that he got rid of this woman. He says that he (Vikram) is a man of honour and should stay away from trouble. As for the money, he says it should not matter to Vikram; he must have already spent lakhs on Purvi. He says Vikram should forget her for his own good. Vikram smiles and thanks him again and rolls up the window.

Jo matlab ka yaar hota hai, woh kisi ke yaar nahin hota ...

Jo paise ka yaar hota hai, woh kisi ka yaar nahin hota ....

Jo karta hai mohabbat khudi se gaafil, Use kisi se pyar nahin hota ....

THE HOME COMING

It has been a long day. A day full of threats, allegations, torture, extortion, money transfers and finally, the compromise. It was as if the entire system had gone against Vikram. The system which normally favours women. The only favourable aspect was Vikram's son and his belief, that he will take his father home. IF IT WAS WAR FOR PURVI AND ANANYA, IT WAS A BATTLE WON FOR AYAAN.

Ayaan is a tough nut to crack. He is a very strong boy emotionally. He has been with Vikram the entire day, and has gone through all the turmoil together with him. He saw him changing guard each time he was confronted with something challenging and frustrating. He kept his cool from outside, but was going through immense turbulence inside; and, he could feel the same happening to him. The emotions were changing every few minutes and that is not normal for perfectly normal people. One thing he was sure of was, that they will come out of this unscathed.

Since childhood, he has seen his father as a very charming man. He has seen his women friends falling head-over-heels in love with him. He has seen him mingling with them, sharing hearty conversations, his poetry, his jokes. But he has never seen him being disrespectful to women. He respected them and never made any sort of advances. He had drawn a line and knew very well never to cross it. This one time, he crossed the line. He sympathized with a woman he was in love with during college days; and, that sympathy became his undoing. But thankfully, his stars helped him overcome this negligence. HE MIGHT BE A GAAFIL, BUT HE IS NOT A KAFIR. He believes in God as much as he believed in his love.

Vikram is driving very slowly. He is physically and mentally exhausted, for he has spent the last six hours of his invaluable time, in a place which would be the last place on earth for any respectable person to visit. And this visit has proved to be once in a lifetime experience. In these six hours, he has seen people falling from grace, falling for money, and failing themselves. He lights up a cigarette and takes a deep drag. He has just come out of HELL.

Ayaan is sitting quietly and watching his father who is silently doing a self-analysis. He knows he will never get over this incident, and he also doubts if he will ever get over with what Purvi has done to him. It is not about losing her; it is about the character she has shown. It is not about the frame-up; it is about the betrayal. For him, it was always about being loyal and trustworthy in a relationship. She was not loyal and she was not trustworthy. He had neglected many of her traits just because he had loved her. He is not hurt by what she has just done to him; he is more hurt by what she had been doing secretly. The loyalty had shifted to some other man (Prakash) and she had ridiculed him (Vikram) for another man.

He is wondering… a woman leaves a man she loves and marries someone of her parents' choice. Then she leaves the man she is married to (Ramit) within seven years of her marriage. Then she meets the man she used to love and has a steady relationship with him (Vikram) for almost seven years. Then she dumps him too for another man (Prakash). IS SHE BLESSED WITH THE SEVEN YEAR ITCH OR NO ONE MAN CURSE!!!!

Ayaan has a lot of questions in mind and he will ask him about them, but first he wants something to eat and drink. So, he asks Vikram to take a stop at a 24/7 convenience store and get some coffee and sandwich. Vikram himself wants to have some cold coffee to lift his depleted spirits. They stop at a store and buy two sandwiches and four coffees. Why four coffees? Two they will have with the sandwich, and two while going home. They don't want to go home right away. There is still some father-son conversation left.

Ayaan asks Vikram: Dad, you are okay, aren't you? Vikram smiles wanly and he gets his answer. How can he be okay? He has just gone through an utmost traumatic experience. But he is curious about a lot of things, so he asks him if there was really a third man in the story. Now, this is one question Vikram himself is struggling to find an answer to. So, he counter-questions: you don't blush for a person if you don't have feelings for him, do you? The next one is, what about the physical intimacy? Vikram knew that sooner or later, this question was bound to come. He wanted to avoid this one, but because he now knows so much about him, he answers it: Son, whatever it was, it was very personal and very pure. I am not ashamed of it and there were no promises. Just an understanding. Understanding of being with each other and for each other. Whatever happened between the two of us was not for the world to know. Not even for you or Ananya. It was foolish and immature of Purvi to share incorrect details with Ananya, and then with Sumer Singh and his colleagues.

The next question is about the will. Ayaan asks Vikram why he was so adamant on getting his name removed from the will. Vikram gets emotional and says: The last time we had an argument, we both were sure that we would not be talking to each other again. But then, we talked; and while talking she told me that even if I was not in her life, I was in her will. So now, when we would not be talking anymore and after whatever we have gone through, I would not like to be associated to her in any form, not even the will. Then, he gets philosophical and says, Moreover, I don't want my name to inflict damage to the will in the future. I want her to live safely and peacefully. Life is a circle, son. What goes around, comes around. She has suffered a lot in life, I don't want her to suffer more because of me. Maybe what happened was for my good. But still, the way she behaved towards the end of the relationship was not right. Next one is not a question, but a statement at large. Ayaan says: Maybe aunty wanted to get rid of you. Maybe she was not getting what she wanted from you. Maybe she wanted you to leave us and live with her. Vikram says he is not sure if this was the reason. He says he still thinks that she wanted to save herself, her image, her character. He is sure that she was cheating on him, he is sure she was two-timing him. It was just that she loved him and was not able to leave him. He says the entire episode was the consequence of him pointing fingers at her character. If he had kept quiet, or said sorry, then things would have remained normal. Ayaan says: You should have said sorry; at least you would not have gone through all this pain.

He finally asks Vikram if he had any regrets about what had happened in the last five days. Vikram says: Not at all. I don't have any regrets whatsoever, about the past, or about the last five days. I loved her, and love has its consequences. Moreover, certain things are not in your hands. The Gods have their own way of telling you that they are supreme. When it was time for you to be together, we gave you those moments. And now when you were supposed to be apart, you are apart. Once again. Ayaan says: Maybe the Gods have given you a closure. The last time, your story was incomplete. Maybe you were not supposed to be together and this is their way of conveying the message. Vikram smiles and says: SO, CLOSURE IT IS. I am lucky that I had a love story. I am lucky to have experienced love. and I will always be thankful to Purvi for being my love. It was all wonderful while it lasted, and she was wonderful till she was. As for being sorry, I can say sorry to her a thousand times, but I am not going to open my arms for her EVER AGAIN!

Sukun ki talash mein, sukun kho diya ....

Sukun jo mila, toh sukun na mila ....